BEREAVED CHILDREN AND TEENS

BEREAVED CHILDREN AND TEENS

A Support Guide for Parents and Professionals

Edited by
EARL A. GROLLMAN

Beacon Press
BOSTON

Beacon Press
25 Beacon Street
Boston, Massachusetts 02108-2892

Beacon Press books
are published under the auspices of
the Unitarian Universalist Association of Congregations.

"I Am," by Aaron Novod, reprinted by permission of Aaron Novod and
Sharon Grollman.

99 98 97 96 95   8 7 6 5 4 3 2 1

Text design by Diane Levy

Library of Congress Cataloging-in-Publication Data

Bereaved children and teens: a support guide for parents and professionals / edited
   by Earl A. Grollman.
      p.   cm.
   Rev. ed. of: Explaining death to children. 1967.
   Includes bibliographical references and index.
   ISBN 0-8070-2306-X
      1. Children and death.   2. Teenagers and death.   3. Bereavement in children.
   4. Bereavement in adolescence.   5. Grief in children.   6. Grief in adolescence.
   I. Grollman, Earl A.   II. Explaining death to children.
   BF723.D3B465   1995
   155.9'37'083—dc20   94-40338
                                                                              CIP

To Jerry,
my brother, my colleague, my friend,
with love and admiration

Contents

Contents

Acknowledgments

I am so fortunate to have as contributors a "dream team" of experts. Each is a renowned authority committed to helping children cope with the inevitability of death. Each is a dear friend of many years. My thanks are incalculable.

To Susan Worst, my Beacon Press editor, I am truly grateful for her sage guidance and sensitive insights and maintaining incredible equanimity despite all the rigors and frustrations of manuscript preparation.

I am indebted to Sharon Grollman for daring to tell her father when his writing was incoherent and then, with thoughtful suggestions, helping resolve the inadequacies.

Susan Rosenburg has always been generous in her conscientious and thoughtful counsel and assistance.

Particular mention must be given to the countless bereaved children who have become my rabbi, my teacher. What a privilege to have been sensitized and educated by them. I now understand the words of the sage: "Much have I learned from my teachers, but more have I learned from my students."

Preface

Sorrow makes us all children again.
— Ralph Waldo Emerson

Almost three decades ago I compiled the book *Explaining Death to Children*. At that time death was a taboo subject. There were but a handful of us who dared consider this topic for scientific inquiry. Most professionals preferred to avoid the issue entirely. Some winced. Others cracked jokes. We ourselves laughingly (but with tears in our eyes) remarked that, if a conference on death were held in the early 1960s, we could *all* meet in a telephone booth. Not infrequently I was referred to by my clergy colleagues as *ha'melech ha'mavet* (in Hebrew, "the angel of death").

So much has occurred in the intervening years. New social forces —the AIDS epidemic, random violent crime, the moral issues of euthanasia and assisted suicide, and the growth of the hospice movement—have jolted society out of the denial of death. Now medical, psychological, and social aspects of death are being openly discussed.

Unfortunately, in too many instances children are *still* the forgotten mourners. For example, recently while conducting a class, a math teacher had a heart attack, fell over, and died. The next day there was a new teacher. The horrendous experience was never once discussed with the students. It was as if the death had never occurred. There are thousands of similar tragedies where children are literally excluded from the grieving process.

Adults may not feel comfortable dealing with children's sadness, especially when they are grieving themselves. They don't know how to start the conversation, they don't know what to say, and, especially, they are fearful of saying the wrong things.

In the film *And We Were Sad, Remember?* when Allison, a seven-year-old girl, first hears of her grandmother's death, she becomes frightened. "Does that mean that other family members will die, too?" Her father "comforts" her: "Little girl, you don't have to worry about that for a hundred years."

But children do worry about death. Traumatic experiences belong to both adulthood and childhood. Anna Quindlen wrote in the *New York Times* that, for people of all ages, "grief remains one of the few things that has the power to silence us. . . . More than sex, grief is unspoken publicly, ignored except for those moments of the funeral that are over too quickly" (4 May 1994).

The authors included here write from a variety of viewpoints and from diverse backgrounds. Yet we share a common goal: to help all children through the most difficult, bewildering, and painful periods of their lives.

We have learned much from each other and from the sorrowing children we have encountered. Dying and death must no longer be considered exclusively X-rated, adult concerns. The modern fields of medicine, psychology, sociology, philosophy, anthropology, religion, and education now offer helpful guidance in explaining death to children. Only when both adults and children can acknowledge and express loss will we find comfort and healing even in the midst of lingering pain and loneliness.

DEATH, DEVELOPMENT, AND RELATIONSHIPS

I Am

I am a bird flying through the sky
I am the tornado ruining a village without pity
I am a monster killing everyone in sight
I am the universe that no one understands
I am a car speeding past everyone
I am a highway with vehicles riding all over me
I am an airplane soaring through the air
I am a sand castle left to be washed away by the tide
I am the sun giving everyone light
I am a noble giving advice to my superior
I am a seed waiting to sprout
I am a weed waiting to take over
I am an earthquake shaking up the earth
I am a snail afraid to come out
I am a cannon shooting out one volley after another
I am firefly a little light of the night
I am anger reaching out at everybody
I am the hope of a newborn baby
I am me
I am me

—Aaron Novod, age eleven
In memory of my teacher, Carol Hantman

Explaining Death to Young Children: Some Questions and Answers

EARL A. GROLLMAN

Children are no strangers to grief. Even infants and toddlers react to loss. When younger children are shielded from death, silence does not take away their pain; it only increases their sense of isolation and abandonment. As adults, we need to understand their concerns, their fantasies, their images of death. We need to acknowledge their fears as real—they are! Above all, we must utilize teachable moments to talk about death in reaching out to children in this, the most profound and far-reaching changes of their lives.

Earl A. Grollman, D.D., is one of the founders of the Good Grief Program, *which provides crisis intervention when a family member, friend, or teacher is terminally ill or dies. His book* Talking about Death: A Dialogue between Parent and Child *received the Unesco award of the International Children and Youth Book exhibition. His other books include* Explaining Death to Children *and* Straight Talk about Death for Teenagers. *Dr. Grollman addresses schools throughout the world.*

Q: Why is it necessary to explain death to young children? If I'm confused about the meaning of death myself, won't I do more harm than good?

A: Many adults say, "Children are too young to understand death. Why burden them with things they cannot possibly grasp?" But children growing up today are all too aware of the reality of death, usually more than adults realize. Even at very young ages, they are confronted with the inevitable moment when life no longer exists: a pet is "put to sleep"; a grandparent dies; a space shuttle explodes; Bambi's mother is killed; a murder is reported on the evening news. Children need adult guidance to make sense of these events.

Traumatized by death, many adults avoid the topic. But avoidance does not make the painful reality go away; by offering children silence and secrecy, adults deny them the opportunity to go through the grieving process with the support of other family members. When, instead, adults talk openly about their own feelings about death, they become role models for their children. And, when children are invited to become part of the mourning process in an accepting and supportive environment, they feel that it is safe to ask questions and share feelings of sadness, anger, guilt, or protest. Only the frank acknowledgment of painful separation, not the denial of tragedy, will lead to good mental health.

Q: But can infants and toddlers really understand death?

A: How children perceive death depends on their age, developmental level, and life experiences, but even very young children try to understand it. From birth to about five years of age, children often conceptualize death as taking a trip or going to sleep. Death is reversible, not permanent—after all, people wake up, and, when going on a trip, they return home again. Death is like the game peek-a-boo, which in Old English meant alive or dead, or like the cartoon characters who miraculously rise up again after being crushed by a speeding train. One three-year-old, whose brother had recently died, kissed her father goodnight, then asked when her brother would be coming back.

But, while they may not understand the permanence of death, young children do react to loss. Changes in the emotional atmosphere of the home and the responses of significant others upset their secure world. Very young children may respond with irritability, variation in crying or eating patterns, and bowel or bladder disturbances. They often regress to behavior that they had outgrown prior to the death, such as thumb-sucking or bed-wetting.

After a death in the family, three- and four-year-olds may be afraid to go to school or even to go to sleep at night. They frequently demand excessive attention from adults, cling to them, follow them around, even climb into bed with them at night. They fear that, if they become separated, either they or their parents will come to harm. Some children are unable to concentrate on their activities, become withdrawn from their friends, and are generally apathetic and depressed.

Q: How about older children? What do they understand?

A: During the elementary school years, children begin to realize that death is final. Unlike younger children, they realize that death is not just another form of life or sleep. But, while children between the ages of five and nine begin to understand the finality of death, they may not always accept it as something that must happen to everyone, particularly to themselves. In addition, some children tend to externalize and personify death, seeing it as an "angel," or "a very old man with a long white beard," or some other figure. Those who watch horror movies and television shows may believe that death is a boogeyman, a skeleton, or a ghost that makes the rounds late at night and selectively carries away helpless victims. Adults need to help children cope with these fears by giving them simple, honest, and accurate information about death.

Around the age of ten, children usually begin to recognize death as a universal and inevitable experience that will occur to them. They also begin to understand that death is not a person but a perceptible end of bodily life. The old magical, life-renewing conception of death is replaced by one that is terminal and fearsome. This perspective carries with it feelings of fragility as young people search for their own identities. When a loved one dies, they may have difficulty concentrating, exhibit a decline in the quality of their schoolwork, become withdrawn and isolated from family and friends, and seem persistently angry and sad. Often they have frequent physical complaints with constant fatigue and frequent drowsiness. (For more information, see chapter 2 by Charles A. Corr.)

Of course, these are general guidelines. Even children of the same age differ widely in their behavior and development. The manner in which children work through their grief depends a great deal on how family members, teachers, and friends reach out to them. The more they are encouraged to share their grief, the more likely that they will be able to cope with the loss in their life.

Q: How can I bring up the subject of death?

A: Since the subject matter is so sensitive, the first discussion should ideally take place before a death occurs and should not concern the eventual death of a specific person close to the child. Don't begin by asking, "Have you ever thought about what you will do when I die?" Such an introduction is security shaking for both adult and child. Similarly, do not couch your explanation in terms of dogma, belief, or theology that is difficult for children to understand. Children easily mistake abstract concepts such as *a higher power* and *the soul* or take literally what is only an idiom, reaching erroneous conclusions. One boy, hearing that God was high and bright, assumed that the weathercock on the barn must be God, for it was the highest and brightest object he knew.

Talking about natural processes is a good way to introduce the concept of death. Change and growth occur each day—from larva to butterfly, from tadpole to frog. New leaves replace the old ones that die. A living tree produces seeds so that life may continue. Point out the diverse forms, shapes, and colors of nature, such as bugs, slugs, and butterflies. Once they moved; after death they are quiet and still. Alternatively, an immediate experience, such as the death of a pet or witnessing death on television, may be a springboard to a discussion about how animals live and die and the sadness that it brings. You should emphasize that, while separation is sad and painful, it is an essential part of life and nature. "There is a time for every living thing to grow and to flourish and then to die" (Eccles. 3:1).

Q: But, when death occurs, what can I say?

A: First, avoid using euphemisms. Don't say that someone has "passed on" or "was lost" or "went away on a long journey." Although they may sound comforting, these statements can be easily misinterpreted. For example, if adults tell children that their loved one went away on a trip, children naturally wonder, "If she was going away, why didn't she even say good-bye? How could she just leave like that?" The deception is further compounded when children see other people mourn: "Why is everyone so sad just because she went away on a trip?" Children may react with anxiety, confusion, and resentment, or they may develop the conviction that someday the loved one will return. To take another example, if adults describe death as "going to sleep," children may develop a pathological dread of bedtime. Some youngsters struggle to stay awake because they fear that, if they fall asleep, they will never wake up again.

Offer theological explanations only with great care. Told that "God took Aunt Ann because he needed her in heaven," a little boy developed a deep resentment against a God who capriciously robbed him of someone he loved. To state that "God wanted him" could make God appear an enemy—vengefully striking the loved one down for being virtuous. (For some ways to discuss religious views of death positively, see chapters 8, 9, and 10.)

If a death occurs, it is important to tell children immediately. If possible, they should be told by a parent or someone close to them. Delay makes it all the more possible that they will be told by the wrong person, at the wrong time, and in the wrong way.

Q: How can I support children who are struggling with death?

A: While insight is a gift, adults must first place themselves in a position to receive it. Be quiet and learn to listen to children; observe their body language, and hear the tone and timbre of their voices. Allow them to talk about death—how they feel, what they think, what they know, and what they want to know. Let them understand that you are trying to comprehend what they are trying to say; answer their questions in the spirit in which they are asked. Children often ask questions to test adults. Hear their questions; try to understand the train of thought leading to the question. Otherwise, the reply may be misleading. What are the children really asking? What do they mean when they ask, "What is going to happen to you, Mommy, when you die?" Are they, in truth, seeking a theological answer, or are they searching for security in their anxiety? Perhaps they want to know, "Who will take care of me?" Or, "Will Daddy die, too, and leave me all alone?" Sometimes the best answers are nonverbal. By holding children close and saying, "All of us hope to go on living together for a long time," you may provide youngsters with the comfort and closeness they need.

Don't be afraid to admit that you don't have all the answers; no adults do. (Children have probably reached this conclusion a long time ago.) It is far healthier for adults and children to seek understanding together than for adults to protect their authority with glib half-truths or evasions. Don't be didactic; leave the door open with such comments as, "Lots of people think about death in different ways, but no one has the final answers. Tell me what you think." Children will both challenge and help you. In your quest to find answers for them, you may discover explanations for yourself. Their doubts may compel you to come to terms with your own thoughts and feelings. When loss is acknowledged and shared, adults and children find comfort in what they mean to each other—even in the midst of lingering pain and loneliness.

Take your time when talking to children about death, and provide opportunities for an ongoing dialogue. Proceed slowly, step by step, listening and responding to children's real concerns and questions. They will fear death less if discussions are focused not only on the details of death but on the beauty of life as well.

There is no single "right" way to tell children about death. Adults should be guided by their own styles, their religious convictions, and what they feel comfortable discussing. Your discussion should correspond to the nature of the death, the children's emotional involvement, and their developmental age.

Explaining Death to Young Children

Q: Do children really grieve?

A: Yes. Grief is an expression of love. Mourning is an appropriate emotion for people of all ages. Children are no strangers to unhappy feelings—they know what it means to feel mad, sad, guilty, lonely, and afraid.

Children's responses to grief fluctuate according to their concepts of death, their developmental level, their relationship with the person who died, the circumstances surrounding the death, and the ability of caregivers to communicate with and emotionally support them. Some children may refuse to speak about the individual who died; others will speak of nothing else. Some will talk of the death at unexpected times —even months and years later. Some will cry uncontrollably; others will remain outwardly impassive and emotionless; others may even laugh. Some will praise the loved one as the most wonderful person in the whole world; others will hate the individual for abandoning them. Some will blame themselves for the death; others will project their grief on God, the physician, the religious leader, the funeral director, or members of the family. Children's despair may be interrupted by a carefree mood, vacillating between sadness and playful joy. Reactions are varied and contradictory—and usually unpredictable.

Children must not be deprived of the right to grieve. They should no more be excluded from sharing grief and sorrow than they should be prevented from demonstrating joy and happiness. Each person, adult and child, should be given the opportunity to lament the end of life in his or her own way. Too often, well-meaning people say, "Be brave! Don't cry! Don't take it so hard." Children should never be discouraged from crying in order to express their grief. Weeping helps express the despair that follows the slow realization that the death is not a bad dream. Don't be afraid to cry in front of children. One of the most loving experiences that adults and children can share is weeping together to express the pain of separation.

Q: What are some of children's emotional reactions to death?

A: Death may bring a variety of emotions.
Denial. "I don't believe it. It didn't happen. It's just a nightmare."

Denial is a natural reaction to loss and takes many forms. Children may look unaffected because they are defending themselves against the terrible loss by pretending that it has not really happened. Disbelief can last for a few hours, or a few weeks, or even a few months. One of the most difficult times for bereaved people of all ages is not at the time of death, when they are surrounded by friends and family; it is months or even years later, when they are finally able to realize that they are indeed alone. It takes time for the full impact of death to penetrate the minds and hearts of survivors. Children may grieve even longer than adults, but perhaps not initially, when there is still a sense of unreality about the death.

Sadness. With the death of a loved one, children may feel more alone than ever. Their own parents, siblings, and friends may be involved in their private worlds of grief, while their loved one is no longer there to share their lives.

Panic. "I have a bump on my neck. I think I have cancer." Children may become preoccupied with the physical symptoms associated with the death of their loved one and feel that they, too, will die of the same illness. They may come to equate death with physical ailments—even slight ones—and hospitals. They think, "Will I die when I have the flu? Or if my head starts to hurt? Or if I have a pain in my arm?"

To help, make a clear distinction between a very serious illness and one that is not life threatening. It may be necessary to repeat again and again, "Even though you and the person who died are in the same family, you are different people. Your doctor has said that you are in good health. You should live for many, many years." Children may also need to be reassured that there is no reason to believe that their parents or other family members will suddenly die. They will not be abandoned.

Guilt. "It's my fault. I should have been nicer." There is a degree of guilt involved in almost every death. It is human to blame oneself for past failures. Guilt takes many forms. It can be manifested outwardly through aggression and hostility: "Why didn't you call the ambulance faster?" By projecting guilt on someone else, children absolve themselves of blame. Or, in an attempt to fight off unhappy thoughts, they may idealize the person, becoming obsessed with only the good qualities of the one who died. They may try to compensate for the loss of a loved one by assuming her characteristics and mannerisms. Guilt may also be turned inward and cause depression. They are no longer able to focus on schoolwork. They are too preoccupied to join others in play. Some cannot sleep, and, when they do, they have recurrent nightmares. Unresolved grief takes the form of withdrawal, delinquency, excessive excitability, self-pity, and defiance.

Children are more likely to feel guilt than adults. In their experience, bad things happen when they are naughty. If they receive good grades, they are rewarded. On the other hand, when they lash out at a sibling, they may be punished. The "desertion" of a loved one is often seen as a retribution for wrongdoing. They search their minds for the "bad thing" for which they are being punished. Scars may last for years. One child, convinced (wrongly) in his own mind that he had caused the death of his sister, suffered years of self-recrimination. Children must understand that nothing they did, said, or thought had anything to do with the death.

Depression. "I don't want to play." "I don't want to eat." "I can't sleep." "Everything feels empty." Suddenly, life seems to have no purpose; the slightest effort leaves one exhausted. Anxiety that expresses itself in physical and emotional symptoms may be brought on by visits from friends or the mere mention of the loved one's name. Each symptom may be experienced alone or in combination and in varying degrees. Whatever the cause, the pain is not imagined. There is no crisis more stressful than the death of a loved one.

Anger. "How could she die?" "Didn't she care enough for me to stay alive?" "Why did he leave me?" "Nothing's the same anymore. She's ruined everything." From denial, children may turn in anger and ask, "Why me?" Bereaved children are often bitter and resentful about their misfortune; they may become irritable and difficult to manage. Don't react to children's anger with threats of punishment. They are experiencing enough guilt and pain already. Approach them with patience and respect. Listen as they tell you about their fears and animosity. If you say, "How can you speak about your poor, dead sister that way?" you only bring the dialogue to an abrupt and unsatisfactory conclusion. Never scold them for feelings, or make them feel ashamed of their emotions, or tell them that they should have only good thoughts about the person who has died. Resentment is a natural part of the grieving process and helps express anguish and frustration at the curtailment of a life so precious. Bottling up anger generates greater stress and leads to depression.

Q: How can I help a child whose parent has died?

A: One of the greatest crises a child can experience is the death of a parent. Never again will the world be as secure a place as it was before. Life is completely disrupted. Youngsters are deprived of the attention and love that they desperately need and want and are filled with anxiety. If you are the child's caregiver, you will hear questions like, "Who will take care of me now?" "Will this happen to you, too?"

The manner in which children cope with this devastating loss depends a great deal on the surviving parent or guardian. If the parent acts as though life is completely unchanged, confused children will try to mimic that attitude, even though it will make them feel even more insecure. If the parent is hostile, intensely anxious, or erratic, children may react similarly. If the parent grieves openly while being consistently loving and reassuring, children will gain the confidence they need to handle the conflicts and changes they are experiencing.

Admittedly, it is difficult for the surviving parent to sustain a sense of family stability, to cope with his or her own loss as well as that of the children. But help is available; support groups and professional counselors can help both parent and youngsters. (See chapter 14 by MaryAnne Schreder.)

If both parents die, special intervention will be needed to help the children cope with their devastating loss. Let them know openly and honestly *where* they will be living and *with whom*. Whenever possible, allow them to participate in important decisions. Give them a listening ear, support, and encouragement. Try not to make changes too rapidly; consistency is especially important when children's lives are changed so drastically. The more freely youngsters are able to express feelings about the past and explore their concerns for the future, the more rapidly they will be able to work through their tremendous grief.

Q: How can I help a child who has lost a brother or a sister?

A: Children are not supposed to die. They are expected to live long, productive lives and grow into old age. With the death of a child, parents as well as siblings are often thrown into crisis. It is difficult for siblings to witness their parents' anguish and inconsolable pain. Yet support for the brothers and sisters of a deceased child is often minimal because family and friends are concerned almost solely with the parents.

With the death of a sibling, children feel more deeply the fragility of life; if their sibling can die, so can they. "Is something wrong with me?" they may wonder. "Will I die when I reach my brother's age?" They may assume a babyish behavior so as magically to prevent themselves from growing old and dying. Adults should say again and again, "You are fine. There is nothing wrong with you. You do *not* have the disease that caused your brother's death."

Seeing the grieving parents, children may try to "replace" the brother or sister and make everything all right again. Adults sometimes unconsciously promote this kind of behavior by saying, "You know, you are so much like him." Parents who do this are hurting themselves and their living children. As difficult as it is to accept, adults must understand that one of their youngsters *is* dead. The child cannot be resurrected in the form of someone else. Don't make comparisons. Surviving children have enough difficulty without having to assume a new identity.

Surviving siblings are often beset with guilt, even more than other grieving children. They remember the times when they fought and argued with the dead sibling. They recall their anger and jealousy. "Is death a punishment for my being bad?" they may question.

Adults must be attuned to the ambiguity of children's feelings—sadness over the loss of a companion and playmate, relief that a competitor is gone, anger over being left out, fear that they are now vulnerable to death. If the death followed a long illness, siblings may have endured months of neglect. The surviving children's ability to cope with their pain will be powerfully influenced by how parents and other adults understand their loss and express their grief. Even though a terrible death has occurred, they are still a family—their love for one another is not lost. (For more information on sibling death, see chapter 5 by Betty Davies.)

Q: How do children react to the death of a grandparent?

A: The death of a grandparent may be the first time that children confront death and witness the grief of those closest to them. Their reactions will depend on the closeness of their relationships. If children didn't know a grandparent well, the effect may be slight. The more their grandparents touched children's lives, the deeper the sorrow they may feel. Bystanders often misguidedly try to offer children comfort by saying, "You're so lucky. Your grandparent lived a long time." Whatever the grandparent's age, assure children that it is okay to mourn; just because the relative who died was aged does not mean that those left behind do not feel a gaping wound in their own lives.

Q: What are the reactions to the death of a friend?

A: When a friend dies, children may suddenly become aware of their own mortality and realize that they, too, can die. Some fear that they might have "caught" the illness. One youngster had an argument with a student who was later killed and felt that he was in some way responsible for the death. Children who have witnessed the death of a classmate may have difficulty returning to the place where the death occurred.

Children can be helped to deal with a friend's death in many ways. In the classroom, teachers, parents, and other concerned adults can help children understand what has occurred by discussing the reason for the now empty chair. Drawing, writing, or dramatic play exercises can help them express their feelings. They may commemorate the event by dedicating the yearbook to, planting a tree in, or placing a bookshelf in the school library in the student's memory. Parents and teachers must remember that effective grief work is not done alone, that the only way *out* of grief is *through* it. (See chapter 13 by Robert G. Stevenson.)

Q: What are reactions to the death of a pet?

A: The death of a pet may be a child's first introduction to a real death. We must allow children to grieve for their pets just as they mourn the loss of human friends and family. Let children participate in the burial of a pet, an opportunity to say good-bye. One child, whose cat was killed by an automobile, gave the burial personal meaning by burying one of her favorite toys with the cat.

Don't rush out too quickly to find a substitute for a dead animal. Wait for the youngsters to mourn their loss before moving on. (See chapter 3 by Kenneth J. Doka.)

Q: Is accidental death more traumatic than other types of death?

A: Yes. The impact of a sudden, accidental death is profound. Survivors—both children and adults—feel an overpowering shock because life is taken away so quickly with no forewarning. They are totally unprepared. Children and adults may continually review the circumstances before the death, playing the final scene over and over again. They think, "If only I could have been there earlier to help." Help children cope with the death by telling them again and again not to punish themselves for something that cannot be changed.

Q: Should children attend the funeral?

A: If children are old enough to attend a service and comprehend in part what is taking place, they should be allowed to attend a ceremony to say farewell to a significant person in their lives.

The funeral is a rite of separation—an acknowledgment that the bad dream is indeed real. Participating helps children understand the finality of death, and it can also help dispel fantasies. The funeral is an opportunity to say good-bye and to acknowledge that the one who died will no longer be part of the familiar environment.

Many children are discomfited by their unfamiliarity with funeral rites and settings. Before attending the funeral, discuss what they might expect. Explain where it will take place. Identify the people who will talk and what they might say. Point out that it can be a strengthening and sharing experience for the entire family.

No matter how helpful and therapeutic the funeral may be, children should never be *forced* to attend. If apprehensive youngsters elect to remain at home, don't pressure them or insinuate that they may not have loved the person who died. Gently suggest that together you might visit the cemetery at another time.

Q: And the cemetery?

A: A funeral does not end in the funeral home or church or synagogue. Its logical conclusion is the grave, the mausoleum, or the columbarium where the loved one is placed. Don't assume that the interment is too traumatic for children. Explain in detail the procedure, and consult them about their wishes and needs. Witnessing the burial may provide a realistic answer to the perennial question, "Where is my loved one's body now?"

Q: How about after the funeral?

A: Just as your children cannot be protected from the knowledge of death, so they cannot and should not be excluded from the grief and mourning that follow the interment. Encourage them to share their emotional experiences with you. Some adults help their children feel needed by asking them to answer the doorbell or telephone after they return from the service. And the presence of a young family member may be the best answer to the bereft adult who questions, "Why should I go on?"

Q: How can we support children when they return to school?

A: After the death of a loved one, children may dread returning to school. They don't know what to expect: how their friends and teachers will react; what they will say or do if someone makes an insensitive remark; what will happen if they burst into tears; and how to go on as if nothing ever happened when it feels like nothing will ever be the same again.

Some children feel better when the class has already learned about the loss. Perhaps a parent or family friend could inform the principal and the child's teachers before he or she returns to school. While children don't want to be singled out and embarrassed, they also don't want to have to play the guessing game "Have they heard?"

Once back at school, children may have difficulty focusing on their work: they may stare aimlessly out the window. If grades begin to slip, they may feel more depressed and inadequate. Some students who have experienced tremendous loss in their lives begin to act out in class. Misconduct, frequent headaches, and stomachaches may be signs that children need counseling.

Q: How much grief is too much?

A: When should adults seek some kind of counseling for their children? Certainly, the need for counseling is difficult to determine during the period immediately following the death. Many people, young and old, say and do things during crises that are not in keeping with their usual behavior. Grief and sorrow leave imprints on the healthiest of personalities.

The line of separation between normal and distorted mourning reaction is thin indeed. The difference is not in the symptom itself but in its intensity, such as continued denial of reality even many months after the funeral; prolonged body distress; persistent frenzy; extended guilt; unceasing apathy; enduring hostile reactions to the one who died and to others. In other words, each manifestation does not in itself indicate a pathological or complicated grief reaction; that can be determined only within the framework of the child's overall behavior.

The question is not only how the child is acting but how long the behavior in question continues. After an initial period of mourning, children are often able to work themselves back to some degree of productive and near-normal living. After several months have elapsed, danger signals may be present if children continue to experience prolonged depression, if their feelings of worthlessness and self-incrimination continue, if they are indifferent to school and activities they once enjoyed, if they are constantly tired or unable to sleep, or if their health suffers markedly. If there are doubts, don't hesitate to seek advice from a therapist, child guidance clinic, school psychologist, or social worker. Receiving professional help is not an admission of weakness but a demonstration of real love and strength. A number of grief support groups are available for children. These groups allow children to share their stories and struggles, offer and receive support from peers, and develop new coping strategies. Through these groups, children learn that they are not alone—there are others who have not only lived through similar situations but prevailed.

Q: How do we help children cope with grief during special days?

A: Special days like the anniversary of a death, birthdays, Mother's or Father's Day, Thanksgiving, and Valentine's Day can be especially difficult for grieving children and adults. Unfortunately, there are no magic formulas to remove suffering. But adults can help children manage the pain on that day by planning ahead and helping them remember their loved one in a meaningful way. Before the event, talk with children about ways you could make the day a less difficult one—perhaps by lighting a candle or planting a tree in memory of the person.

Q: What else can we do to help children?

A: If you are experiencing the death of a close family member, a desire to run away is natural. But memories cannot, and should not, be denied. Avoid making any abrupt, final decisions immediately following the death of a loved one. Many people leave the security of familiar surroundings only to discover that problems are intensified rather than diminished. Children especially need to retain roots in the same neighborhood with longtime playmates. And they need to remember. Don't attempt to eradicate the memory of a loved one. Give children pictures and tangible reminders to help them remember their loved one.

The greatest gift that you can give to your children is yourself. When you talk with them, or when they talk to you, stop, if possible, what you are doing; give them your undivided attention. Remember, they are different from you and react and understand death in their own ways. Use "openers" that invite them to talk about the crisis in their life: "Say that again. I want to be sure I understand you. Tell me more." Move physically closer to them. Gently touch them and say their name. Respond with patience and understanding. Speak in a quiet, caring voice. Praise them when they share their innermost thoughts. And always remember that children are never too old, or too young, to be told that they are loved.

Q: What can adults do to help themselves?

A: Talking about death is often a complex and disturbing task. In the end, what you feel will determine what you teach. If you are continually agitated, children will feel your anxieties and tensions. Regardless of the words you use, your emotions will show through.

By dealing with your own grief, you will learn to accept death, and acceptance will help you and the children start to build a bridge to span that chasm with the things of life that still count—memory, family, friendship, love. Most important—for adults and children—is the knowledge that life continues despite pain. Grief is a strange mixture of joy and sorrow—joy to be alive and sorrow to have life diminished by the loss of one you love. As you walk together on the long and difficult path of separation, you will find new dimensions of caring, understanding, and healing.

You will stop at different places along the journey; some may linger longer, and most will vacillate among the rest points of grief. The journey may never end completely. But healing begins when you remember the life more than the death. You may always be bereaved, but you need not be in constant grief. Recovery and growth are possible!

Chapter Two

Entering into Adolescent Understandings of Death

CHARLES A. CORR

Rainer Maria Rilke, the German poet laureate, observed that there are many small deaths in a person's life. This is especially true for adolescents. There is the death of their early childhood as they struggle between wanting to be independent and fearing separation. When adolescents experience the death of a family member, a friend, a teacher, they are often left even more bewildered in their search for identity. How can we help them find understanding, guidance, and support when the road ahead is so uncertain?

Charles A. Corr, Ph.D., is professor, School of Humanities, Southern Illinois University at Edwardsville. From 1989 to 1993 he was chair of the International Work Group on Death, Dying, and Bereavement. His publications include Helping Children Cope with Death: Guidelines and Resources *(2d ed., 1984),* Childhood and Death *(1984),* Hospice Approaches to Pediatric Care *(1985),* Adolescence and Death *(1986),* Sudden Infant Death Syndrome: Who Can Help and How *(1991), and* Death and Dying, Life and Living *(1994).*

This chapter explores how adolescents perceive and understand death. It responds to such questions as, What are the principal elements that enter into adolescent understandings of death? Are the important variables solely cognitive, or are there other salient factors? How can adults help adolescents understand death?

First, we need to explore contrasts between adult and adolescent perspectives on adolescence itself, ways in which adolescents are and are not alike, and some facts about contemporary patterns of adolescent encounters with death in our society.

Adolescents and Adults

To most adults, adolescents are interesting, but often puzzling and challenging. Adults see in these young people individuals who are vibrantly alive, growing, and becoming like their older counterparts. Adolescents are youngsters who have outgrown many of the limitations and restrictions of childhood and who are in the process of developing into young adults. To most adults, adolescents enjoy a special freedom because they have not yet assumed all the burdens and responsibilities of adulthood.

Adolescents are, nevertheless, puzzling and challenging to adults as well. First, they often seem to separate or distance themselves from the adults around them and from adult rules, in part because their desire to conform to the customs and standards of peers is often extremely important. As Ryan White (White and Cunningham 1991, 3) has written, "All I ever wanted to do was be one of the kids because that's what counts in high school." Ryan referred to the HIV infection and AIDS that brought him so much unwanted attention and eventually took his life, but his point is valid in a more general way. Teenagers often draw back from adults and turn to peers, and this requires that adults give adolescents the psychosocial space and tolerance that they need to develop in healthy ways. At the same time, adults must continue to provide the sense of connectedness, support, discipline, and structure that adolescents also need.

Second, adolescents do not always view their own situation in the same ways that adults do. Adolescents are often preoccupied with their own everyday burdens and with the myriad developmental changes that they are experiencing. In these circumstances, adolescents do not have the luxury and the benign distortions of hindsight that are often found in adults. Consequently, the story that adults tell to themselves and to the adolescents around them about the adolescent years may not be wholly congruent with the story that adolescents tell (or fail to tell) to themselves, to their peers, and to adults.

How Are Adolescents Alike and Not Alike?

In order to enter into the milieu of adolescents, it is important to recognize some of the many ways in which adolescents are alike as well as some of the many ways in which they differ. For example, the word *adolescence* encompasses many individuals, all of whom have attained different levels of development. In general, *adolescents* are somewhere in between childhood and adulthood. But these "in between" people differ among themselves in significant ways.

In American society, youngsters who are thirteen or fourteen may be just settling into junior high or middle school. Most people who are sixteen or seventeen will have gone on to high school and may be driving or working part-time. And those who are eighteen or nineteen may have graduated from high school (or dropped out) and gone on to college or a full-time job.

According to Fleming and Adolph (1986), the youngest of these three groups is likely to be especially concerned with achieving emotional separation from parents, while the next group will be striving toward competency, mastery, and control, and the last group will be seeking to reestablish intimacy and commitment. In short, early, middle, and late adolescents are likely to find themselves facing different developmental tasks in differing developmental conditions.

Adolescents may also differ in other ways. Many of the features of their lives—the places in which they live, the cultures within which they find themselves, the racial, ethnic, or religious features of their families and immediate environments—may be special or distinctive. Adolescents around the globe may know war or peace, famine or plenty, advanced technology or a simple life. In the United States alone, adolescents may live in safety or in a world of violence, in urban masses or rural spaces, in artificial environments or close to nature. To be an adolescent in the late twentieth century is to be not an abstraction but a real person living in a specific place and at a specific developmental level.

When it comes to coping with stressors like death, adolescents manage challenges in different ways. The challenges themselves will be different, as will the relationships or attachments that are disrupted. Similarly, individual adolescents will differ in their personalities and in the ways in which they have learned to cope throughout the early years of their lives.

Perhaps there are only two things that can really be said to be common to adolescents who are coping with death. First, they are all human beings. As such, adolescents share with all other human beings a complex life form—one in which physical, psychological, social, and spiritual dimensions constantly interact—and a desire to live as well as they can. Second, adolescents are generally those human beings for whom the developmental tasks involved in establishing a relatively stable sense of personal identity are of particular importance.

Adolescent Encounters with Death

In the United States in recent years, adolescents have occupied a privileged position in relation to encounters with death. First, overall death rates (87.9 per 100,000 in 1990, the most recent year for which reliable data are currently available) are low during the middle and later adolescent years. This figure is not as low as death rates in middle childhood (22.0 per 100,000 for ages five to nine years) or for later childhood and the early adolescents years (26.0 per 100,000 for ages ten to fourteen years). But it is markedly lower than those in infancy or in any subsequent period during the adult years (NCHS 1993).

Second, adolescence (a period considered in many official demographic documents as including those who are fifteen to twenty-four years of age) is the only era in the entire human life span during which some "natural cause" does not appear among the three leading causes of death. Some adolescents do die of malignant neoplasms (cancer) and diseases of the heart. These are the fourth and fifth leading causes of death, respectively, for the adolescent population in our society during recent years. But in each case the numbers and rates for these deaths are relatively low. As a group, most adolescents are healthy people who have survived the dangers in childhood of death from natural causes and who have not yet lived long enough to be threatened by the specter of degenerative diseases that dominates death among adults.

Third, the three leading causes of death among adolescents in the United States in 1990 were accidents (almost 78 percent of which involved motor vehicles), homicides, and suicides (NCHS 1993). All these are human-induced deaths. In other words, they are deaths caused by adolescents themselves or by others around them. Together they account for nearly 80 percent of all adolescent deaths. (Note that the way in which demographic statistics like this are organized influences subsequent descriptions. For example, suicide is the third leading cause of death for individuals who are fifteen to twenty-four years of age but the second leading cause of death for those fifteen to nineteen years of age.)

Fourth, adolescents in the United States are in growing danger of dying from conditions associated with the human immunodeficiency virus (HIV) and its end state, acquired immunodeficiency syndrome (AIDS). In fact, by 1990 HIV infection had become the sixth leading cause of death among adolescents (NCHS 1993).

This brief description of adolescent encounters with death has several immediate implications. First, most adolescents in our society will not die; they will live on into adulthood. Second, those adolescents who do die of human-induced causes will often die in relatively sudden and unexpected ways. Their peers will be given little warning or time to prepare for these deaths. And these deaths will often be associated with trauma and violence. Third, adolescents who encounter death as a result of homicide, suicide, or HIV infection will often find such deaths to be associated with ways in which they or others around them have chosen to cope with the stressors in their lives. This element of choice and undesirable or ineffective coping behaviors is often a complicating factor in the bereavement that follows such deaths.

Adolescents are also the first developmental group that is able to encounter the full range of cross-generational deaths. Like children, adolescents may experience the deaths of parents, grandparents, and other adults. But, unlike most children, adolescents may also experience the deaths both of younger siblings and of their own offspring. Adolescents who become bereaved parents are a special group, one about which we still have much to learn (Barnickol, Fuller, and Shinners 1986).

Adolescent Understandings of Death

Understanding the Concept as Opposed to the Significance of Death

Some children may not be able to understand the concept of death or may be able to understand only some aspects of that concept (e.g., its finality but not its universality). Normally developing adolescents, however, are capable of understanding the concept of death in mature or adult ways. This statement may seem to imply that the major transition in developing understandings of death is between the cognitive capacities of childhood and those of adolescence. Were this true, the only important factor would be the capacity to think in an abstract way, and there would be no essential differences between the ways in which adolescents and adults can or do think about death. In fact, that is not correct.

Normally developing adolescents can think about death in an abstract, conceptual, formal, mature, scientific, or adult way. That fact on its own does not necessarily mean that they actually or even frequently do think about death in those ways. To have the ability to think in a certain way is not the same as actually thinking in that way. The import of this can be illustrated in various ways.

For example, in one research study (Alexander and Adlerstein 1958), 108 boys between the ages of five and sixteen years were asked to engage in a word association test in which three death-related words (*buried*, *kill*, and *dead*) were included in a set of twenty-seven stimulus words. Decreased speed of response and decreased galvanic skin resistance (associated with increased perspiration) were interpreted as reflecting heightened anxiety. Scoring results displayed a bimodal distribution. Those who were five to eight years old and thirteen to sixteen years old had higher scores than those who were nine to twelve years old.

On the surface, this is somewhat surprising. One might have expected increasing conceptual awareness of death to be either directly or inversely associated with anxiety about death. That is, greater understanding might have led to lessened anxiety because of the element of increased personal control implied in the ability to form and work with abstract concepts. Alternatively, greater understanding might have led to heightened anxiety because of increasing awareness of the finality and universality implicit in the content of one's concept of death. In fact, the researchers concluded that "death has a greater emotional significance for people with less stable ego self-pictures than for people with an adequate concept of the self" (Alexander and Adlerstein 1958, 175). This is relevant both to children who are five to eight years old and confronting challenges in their early school years and to adolescents for whom, as we have seen, ego stability and identity are precisely the central developmental issues.

In other words, that an adolescent is able to understand or actually does understand that all human beings are mortal is not the same as the realization that the attribute of mortality applies to himself or herself. Thus, Tolstoy (1884/1960, 131) wrote the following about Ivan Ilych: "The syllogism he had learnt from Kiezewetter's Logic: 'Caius is a man, men are mortal, therefore Caius is mortal' had always seemed to him correct as applied to Caius, but certainly not as applied to himself." Instead of grasping the personal significance of mortality, the adolescent Ivan was content merely to note that the abstract concept *mortality* was somehow joined or linked to the equally abstract or distanced notion *Caius* (or, perhaps, *humanity*). For Ivan Ilych, it took a life-threatening event and the experience of his own dying to break through this distanced and abstract concatenation of concepts. What would it take for an adolescent in our society to grasp the implications of his or her own personal mortality?

Adolescents and Children, Adolescents versus Children

These examples from scientific research and imaginative fiction show the dangers of isolating cognitive capacity from the rest of the human being and reveal interesting similarities and differences between child-hood and adolescence. It is often said that an egocentric perspective serves to protect children from grasping the full implications of their mortality. If anyone is to die, it will be the other, not the child. Thus, peek-a-boo is a game in which the rest of the world disappears (dies?) and reappears. Whether this threatens or delights the child depends on his or her personality and perception of these events. But the contin-ued existence of the child throughout the game of peek-a-boo is not questioned.

Gordon (1986) has suggested that some remnants of what she called the "tattered cloak of immortality" may carry over at least into early adolescence. And Elkind (1967) has reported that many adolescents are engrossed in their own "personal fable," the excitement and vitality of an individual life story that may blind them (at least in some degree) to the threat that death might cut short the telling of this tale. If these commentators are correct, as they seem to be, then there are compel-ling forces at work in adolescent life that militate against the willing-ness and ability of adolescents to grasp the significance of their own mortality.

An interesting analysis of driving patterns in later adolescence (Jo-nah 1986) seems to confirm this account of adolescent perceptions and understandings of death. As is well known, adolescent drivers are at much higher risk of being involved in accidents than older drivers. Why is this so? Jonah has suggested two central reasons. First, adoles-cent drivers may simply not perceive the risks that they are taking as dangerous. They may not grasp the likelihood that an accident might occur in a given set of circumstances or that it might result in serious consequences. Consequently, they may drive thoughtlessly into situa-tions that older drivers would be more likely to avoid or to approach with greater caution. Second, adolescent drivers may find positive value or personal utility in taking certain risks. For example, the very act of driving an automobile or of driving in certain ways may be a way of asserting one's independence, expressing opposition to author-ity, coping with frustration, or gaining the acceptance of peers.

The first of these is a matter of risk perception, the second one of risk utility. Deficiencies in risk perception are counteracted by broadened experience and heightened awareness; distortions in risk utility are counteracted by increased maturation and improved coping skills. Until inadequacies in risk perception and/or risk utility are corrected, it should not seem surprising that "death is a very remote event for most young people" (Jonah 1986, 268).

Noppe and Noppe (1991) have approached this issue in a broader way by suggesting that there are four dialectical themes that highlight what they have described as "the ambiguous relationship with death that appears to be characteristic of the adolescent years" (p. 31). By "dialectical themes" Noppe and Noppe mean biological, cognitive, social, and affective tensions within adolescent life that may possibly have to do with death.

For example, according to Noppe and Noppe, while adolescence is a time of vibrant *biological* transformation and physical development, all those changes may also be associated with an awareness of the loss of a simpler, more innocent past (prepubertal asexuality) and the inevitability of biological decline leading ultimately to the death of oneself and others. Similarly, for Noppe and Noppe, the *cognitive* dialectic involves enhanced abilities to think about the future—which includes both positive and negative aspects, both life and death—and against which one may prefer to immerse oneself intensely in the present (Kastenbaum 1959). Likewise, changing *social* relationships with family members and peers may involve both opportunities for growth and dangers of social losses in the form of "little deaths," while *affective* tensions may be found within the processes of adolescent separation and individuation. This account of four types of dialectical tensions within the adolescent years and a potentially ambiguous relation with death need not be accepted in all its details for one to appreciate parallels with other analyses of adolescent life and to concede the underlying premise that growth such as that which typifies the adolescent years embodies elements of both affirmation and loss.

Indeed, Sugar (1968) has described "normal adolescent mourning" as involving processes of protest/searching, disorganization, and reorganization. What is perhaps most significant about this account are the similarities that it bears to Fleming and Adolph's (1986) description of characteristic developmental tasks during adolescence: establishing emotional separation, achieving competency or mastery, and reestablishing intimacy. Both developmental and situational (in this case, grief-related) tasks in adolescence involve confronting and coping with challenges that have notable aspects of resemblance. Perhaps that is why it is often difficult to untangle precisely what is at issue when an adolescent is grieving. Nevertheless, it is in the ongoing negotiation of these challenges and the cultivation of appropriate coping skills that adolescents must live and can live most successfully. Or, as Raphael (1983, 147) has described the results of a study by Maurer (1964), for adolescents maturation is associated with "greater sophistication and acknowledgement of the inevitability of death as well as with enjoyment of life and altruistic concerns."

Helping Adolescents Cope with Death

Many adults believe that it is difficult to help adolescents cope with death because adolescents are reputed to turn away from adults and to talk only with other adolescents. This may be true, but it is not the whole story. In the first place, parents and other adults help adolescents by teaching and modeling various sorts of coping behaviors. Adults also influence in prominent ways the situations within which adolescents find themselves, such as neighborhoods, schools, and religious and other groups. As they become more independent of their parents and other family members, adolescents may move into new and different situations. But enlarging the world in which adolescents live out their lives is not necessarily the same as abandoning (wholly or in part) its original shape and authority.

Moreover, both the peers to whom adolescents turn and the other adults who become influential in their lives (e.g., teachers, counselors, religious leaders) are again individuals who have come on the scene in part as a result of parents' choices. The degree to which such choices remain influential in the lives of adolescents and the specific ways in which those influences work themselves out may vary as adolescents exercise their own freedom and choose their own paths. New and different elements enter into the lives of adolescents at different points and in different ways, but adolescent life is never completely a creation from nothing.

In this context, parents and other significant adults can play their most constructive roles by maintaining open and healthy lines of communication with adolescents. This requires adults to take an interest in the lives of adolescents, to make active efforts to reach out to adolescents, and to listen attentively to the concerns of adolescents. Like all human beings, adolescents may communicate their concerns through words (in both literal and symbolic ways) and through behaviors. One must not only listen to the surface meanings of these communications but also watch for hidden or underlying factors that may be closer to the central points at issue.

In our society, when adolescents turn to peers in order to seek help in coping with death, they may often find that their peers have no significant resources to offer. Having little experience with death-related situations, other adolescents may not know what to say or do to help a friend in such matters. Sometimes, however, adolescent peers can draw on a reservoir of prior experiences with loss or on natural sensitivity and helping skills. In some areas, adolescents have been shown how to be peer counselors who can listen and assist with processes of problem solving. Similarly, some organizations (e.g., schools, religious groups, or health-care providers) have founded support groups for adolescents who have experienced death or loss. One of the earliest of these was established in 1979 in a school district in Mississauga, Ontario (a suburb of Toronto) (Baxter, Bennett, and Stuart 1987). Another program called Teen Age Grief has helped establish school-based programs in California (Cunningham 1990). And an impressive range of center-based programs for both children and adolescents is conducted at the Dougy Center in Portland, Oregon (Corr et al. 1991). Within these nonjudgmental, mutual-aid, self-help groups, adolescents can share their grief and acquire useful information about coping with loss.

Still another way to help adolescents who are coping with death involves "bibliotherapy" or the use of books as aids to personal coping. A growing body of literature—both fiction and nonfiction—for adolescents describes many different kinds of loss. Five examples of this sort of literature are *Bridge to Terabithia* (Paterson 1977), *Say Goodnight, Gracie* (Deaver 1988), *Shira: A Legacy of Courage* (Grollman 1988), *The Sunday Doll* (Shura 1988), and *Tiger Eyes* (Blume 1981). Literature such as this helps "normalize" loss, acknowledge the reality of loss, diminish the sense of estrangement or alienation that often accompanies loss, and identify, validate, and suggest constructive outlets for strong reactions to loss. Whether fiction or nonfiction, good resources encourage adolescents to learn from the experiences of others and to work out their own solutions to life's challenges.

Bibliotherapy can even be useful for adolescents with limited reading skills. A wide range of literature is available, including picture books and very simple stories, that is suitable for readers at all levels. This body of literature is so broad and diverse that one might do well to begin by consulting existing guides in the field (e.g., Corr 1993; Bernstein and Rudman 1989). Adults can simply make these titles available to adolescents who may need them, or they can offer to read and discuss a particular book along with them. A project of this sort can even be made less personal and less threatening by framing it as an invitation to assist the adult in assessing the appropriateness of selected titles in this field for younger readers. In this way, the adolescent is a colleague and an adviser, whose personal involvement and potential benefit are not singled out and forced onto center stage.

Adolescents who are open to writing, art, drama, or other modes of expression can be invited to address loss and grief in these ways. Keeping a journal, drawing a picture, writing a letter, creating a collage, composing a poem, paging through a scrapbook, or acting out a scene can all be useful ways in which to assist coping with loss. Adults may come along on such journeys or share the results; however, they should take care to follow the lead of the adolescent, to respect a desire to keep the work private, and to permit the adolescent to interpret the content and significance of the project in his or her own way.

Conclusion

Adolescents cannot avoid all encounters with loss and death. These experiences are a part of living in our society and in every society. In our society, however, deaths of adolescents are likely to be sudden, unanticipated, violent, and traumatic. And adolescents may not have much experience with or effective preparation for coping with these or other sorts of losses and deaths. Thus, death–related encounters may present special challenges to adolescents in our society, precisely at the point when they are striving to establish their own sense of a stable personal identity.

By contrast with children, most normally developing adolescents can conceptualize death in abstract and adult ways. However, for both developmental and situational or experiential reasons, many adolescents may be reluctant to think of death in this way. It may be especially difficult for these youngsters to think of death as something that will eventually happen to them. Adults can assist in that process by taking the initiative to enter into the world of adolescent understandings of death, by listening carefully to and being supportive of individual adolescents as they struggle to balance a recognition of the meaning of death with an appreciation of the good in life, and by sharing with adolescents in a constructive way the insights that life experiences have taught them about coping with loss and death.

In much of this, the proper focus is not just on a unidirectional process in which an adult helps an adolescent but rather on a mutual exchange in which both adult and adolescent share concerns, reactions, and coping processes. The reason for this is that coping with loss and death is not a matter in which wisdom belongs exclusively to adults. All human beings have much to share with (and thus to learn from) each other about what a loss or a death has meant, what it has stimulated, and what it might lead to. Adults who are open to this sort of exchange will soon realize that adolescents often have much to contribute.

References

Alexander, I. E., and A. M. Adlerstein. 1958. "Affective Responses to the Concept of Death in a Population of Children and Early Adolescents." *Journal of Genetic Psychology* 93:167–77.

Barnickol, C. A., H. Fuller, and B. Shinners. 1986. "Helping Bereaved Adolescent Parents." In *Adolescence and Death*, ed. C. A. Corr and J. N. McNeil, 132–47. New York: Springer.

Baxter, G., L. Bennett, and W. Stuart. 1987. *Adolescents and Death: Bereavement*

Support Groups for Secondary School Students—a Practitioner's Manual. 2d ed. Etobicoke, Ont.: Canadian Centre for Death Education and Bereavement at Humber College.

Bernstein, J. E., and M. K. Rudman. 1989. *Books to Help Children Cope with Separation and Loss.* Vol. 3. New York: Bowker.

Blume, J. 1981. *Tiger Eyes.* Scarsdale, NY: Bradbury.

Corr, C. A. 1993. "Children's Literature on Death." In *Hospice Care for Children*, ed. A. Armstrong-Dailey and S. Z. Goltzer, 266–84. New York: Oxford University Press.

Corr, C. A., et al. 1991. "Support for Grieving Children: The Dougy Center and the Hospice Philosophy." *American Journal of Hospice and Palliative Care* 8, no. 4:23–27.

Cunningham, L. 1990. *Teen Age Grief: A Training Manual for Initiating and Facilitating Grief Support Groups for Teens.* Panorama City, Calif.: Teen Age Grief.

Deaver, J. R. 1988. *Say Goodnight, Gracie.* New York: Harper & Row.

Elkind, D. 1967. "Egocentrism in Adolescence." *Child Development* 38: 1025–34.

Fleming, S. J., and R. Adolph. 1986. "Helping Bereaved Adolescents: Needs and Responses." In *Adolescence and Death*, ed. C. A. Corr and J. N. McNeil, 97–118. New York: Springer.

Gordon, A. K. 1986. "The Tattered Cloak of Immortality." In *Adolescence and Death*, ed. C. A. Corr and J. N. McNeil, 16–31. New York: Springer.

Grollman, S. 1988. *Shira: A Legacy of Courage.* New York: Doubleday.

Jonah, B. A. 1986. "Accident Risk and Risk-Taking Behaviour among Young Drivers." *Accident Analysis and Prevention* 18, no. 4:255–71.

Kastenbaum, R. 1959. "Time and Death in Adolescence." In *The Meaning of Death*, ed. H. Feifel, 99–113. New York: McGraw-Hill.

Maurer, A. 1964. "Adolescent Attitudes toward Death." *Journal of Genetic Psychology* 105:75–90.

National Center for Health Statistics (NCHS). 1993. "Advance Report of Final Mortality Statistics, 1990." *Monthly Vital Statistics Report*, vol. 41, no. 7 (suppl.). Hyattsville, MD: U.S. Department of Health and Human Services, Public Health Service, Centers for Disease Control and Prevention.

Noppe, L. D., and I. C. Noppe. 1991. "Dialectical Themes in Adolescent Conceptions of Death." *Journal of Adolescent Research* 6:28–42.

Paterson, K. 1977. *Bridge to Terabithia.* New York: Crowell.

Raphael, B. 1983. *The Anatomy of Bereavement.* New York: Basic.

Shura, M. F. 1988. *The Sunday Doll.* New York: Dodd, Mead.

Sugar, M. 1968. "Normal Adolescent Mourning." *American Journal of Psychotherapy* 22:258–69.

Tolstoy, L. 1960. *The Death of Ivan Ilych and Other Stories* (1884). Translated by A. Maude. New York: New American Library.

White, R., and A. M. Cunningham. 1991. *Ryan White: My Own Story.* New York: Dial.

Suggested Readings

For General Readers

Bode, J. 1993. *Death Is Hard to Live With: Teenagers and How They Cope with Death.* New York: Delacorte.

Gordon, A. K., and D. Klass. 1979. *They Need to Know: How to Teach Children about Death.* Englewood Cliffs, NJ: Prentice-Hall.

Gravelle, K., and C. Haskins. 1989. *Teenagers Face to Face with Bereavement.* New York: Julian Messner.

Grollman, E. A. 1993. *Straight Talk about Death for Teenagers: How to Cope with Losing Someone You Love.* Boston: Beacon.

Krementz, J. 1981. *How It Feels When a Parent Dies.* New York: Knopf.

Krementz, J. 1989. *How It Feels to Fight for Your Life.* Boston: Little, Brown.

LeShan, E. 1978. *Learning to Say Good-By: When a Parent Dies.* New York: Macmillan.

Pendleton, E., comp. 1980. *Too Old to Cry, Too Young to Die: 35 Teenagers Talk about Cancer.* Nashville: Thomas Nelson.

Sternberg, F., and B. Sternberg. 1980. *If I Die and When I Do: Exploring Death with Young People.* Englewood Cliffs, NJ: Prentice-Hall.

For More Specialized Readers

Balk, D. E., ed. 1991. *Journal of Adolescent Research*, vol. 6, no. 1. (Special issue on death and adolescent bereavement.)

Corr, C. A., and J. N. McNeil. 1986. *Adolescence and Death.* New York: Springer.

LaGrand, L. 1986. *Coping with Separation and Loss as a Young Adult: Theoretical and Practical Realities.* Springfield, Ill.: Charles C. Thomas.

Offer, D., E. Ostrov, and K. I. Howard. 1981. *The Adolescent: A Psychological Self-Portrait.* New York: Basic.

Offer, D., E. Ostrov, and K. I. Howard, eds. 1984. *Patterns of Adolescent Self-Image.* San Francisco: Jossey-Bass.

Chapter Three

Friends, Teachers, Movie Stars: The Disenfranchised Grief of Children

KENNETH J. DOKA

For children, grief is composed of a million moments of broken connections. They may feel empowered to express their emotions when a loved one has died but not for other significant losses, such as moving to another neighborhood, a divorce in the family, or, in adolescence, a failed romance. They need us to help them find the courage to address the hidden despair, their disenfranchised grief, for loss is a lifelong human condition.

Kenneth J. Doka, Ph.D., is professor of gerontology at the College of New Rochelle. He is the author of three books, Disenfranchised Grief: Coping with Hidden Sorrow, Living with Life-Threatening Illness, *and* Death and Spirituality. *In addition, he has written more than forty articles on aging, dying, and grief. In 1993 he was elected president of the Association of Death Education and Counseling.*

One of the perennial debates in psychology is the question of when children are capable of grief. According to some, particularly those who take a psychoanalytic approach, true mourning does not occur until a child has fully developed an identity in adolescence. Others hold that children are capable of grief once they achieve object consistency, around the age of three. I have always liked psychologist William Worden's (1991) comment—that *all* children are capable of grief but that they express (handle) their grief in different ways than adults.

Worden's position affirms two major points. First, it reminds us that from the earliest ages children form attachments and can experience significant loss when these attachments are severed. Second, it also recognizes that children are still developing—cognitively, emotionally, spiritually, behaviorally. Hence, they are likely to express their grief differently at different stages of their development.

But, even if we understand and recognize that children do grieve, we do not always acknowledge all their losses. Like adults, sometimes children's grief is disenfranchised; although they grieve, others around them do not acknowledge their right to mourn.

This chapter explores the disenfranchised grief of children. Beginning with a brief overview of the concept of disenfranchised grief, I then consider the types of losses that children may experience that might be disenfranchised. Finally, I offer suggestions for helping children cope with disenfranchised grief.

Disenfranchised Grief

In every society there are norms or rules that regulate behavior. From the time we are born, we are constantly taught these rules—how and what to eat, ways to dress, how to behave toward other people.

But we learn other sets of rules as well—"feeling" rules that govern the ways we are expected to feel. We make reference to these rules all the time. "I have every right to feel angry." "I know I shouldn't feel guilty." In each of these situations, feeling rules are evoked that affirm or contrast our own feelings with some accepted norm.

Some of these feeling rules define who, what, when, and how someone is supposed to grieve. In most Western societies, these norms define *grief* narrowly. We have a right to grieve when family members die; in many businesses, workers are accorded time off when members of the immediate family die.

Yet our attachments extend beyond the family. But, when we grieve the loss of those loved ones, our grief is likely to be disenfranchised; it is not openly acknowledged, socially supported or sanctioned, or publicly shared. Sometimes one may disenfranchise oneself out of shame or guilt. For example, a man involved in an extramarital affair may never be able to acknowledge the relationship or his grief over the loss should his lover die. Even if he did, others may not acknowledge his right to grieve.

In an earlier book, *Disenfranchised Grief* (1989), I described four different contexts of disenfranchised grief. The first context includes unrecognized relationships. In many relationships outside kin, the closeness of the attachment is often not appreciated. The loss of a friend or a lover, for example, may be devastating, yet at best the friend may be expected to support family members. Death can even engender grief when it ends relationships that existed in the past (e.g., that with an ex-spouse) or never involved actual interactions (that with a celebrity).

A second context of disenfranchised grief involves losses that are not recognized as significant. Abortion, perinatal loss, the loss of a pet, all can be grieved. Many non-death-related losses such as incarceration, divorce, adoption, or placement in foster care may cause grief reactions that are unrecognized by others.

In the third context, grievers are not recognized as being capable of feeling grief. The grief of the very young, the very old, or the mentally or developmentally impaired is often unacknowledged. Fourth, certain types of deaths can be so shameful that even grievers with a socially legitimate right to grieve may be reluctant to acknowledge their loss. Examples of disenfranchising deaths include suicide, alcohol- or drug-related deaths, or victim-precipitated homicide. Given the stigma attached to the disease, many grievers may feel that they cannot publicly acknowledge the loss of someone who died of AIDS, depriving themselves of the opportunity to mourn or seek support.

Whatever the context, each of these losses shares one similar characteristic. In each there is a sense that those experiencing the loss have no right to grieve. Their grief is disenfranchised.

The Disenfranchised Grief of Children

Like adults, children, too, can be disenfranchised grievers, often for the very same reasons. Like the rest of us, children have a circle of people with whom they are exceedingly close. Friends are an extremely important part of their social world. Writing in his novella *The Body* (which later became the basis for the 1986 movie *Stand by Me*), Stephen King reflects that we never have friendships as strong as those in childhood. Perhaps it is because adults simply do not have the time for friendships that children do. Children and adolescents can literally spend scores of hours each week developing, maintaining, and nurturing their ties.

The death of a friend can be devastating. Not only is it a frightening reminder of vulnerability and mortality, but it is also the loss of a key relationship, a part of the child's identity. Children will grieve these losses intensely. But the adults around them may not recognize the great significance of the loss. In one case, for example, Joey's parents were deeply troubled by the fact that their nine-year-old son seemed to accept the loss of his grandmother so well but was devastated when his friend Todd drowned on vacation. They failed to recognize that, while his grandmother played only a small part in his life, Todd was one of Joey's most significant ties. From daily rides to school to weekend sleep overs to after-school sports, Joey and Todd were inseparable. Teachers, coaches, neighbors, and supportive adults may also be part of the child's world, and children may grieve their deaths deeply as well.

Relationships with noncustodial parents are also likely to be more significant than others recognize. I investigated the reactions of children to the deaths of their noncustodial parents, particularly parents who had had minimal connection to the child. Many of these children did feel grief, not only for the death of their natural parent, but also for the ties that never had an opportunity to develop. Mark is a good example of this. Mark was not yet born when his parents divorced. His father never saw him or even acknowledged him as his son. When his father died ten years later, Mark's mother could not understand her son's grief. Mark grieved the relationship that never was and now never would be. With his father's death, Mark's fantasy of an eventual reconciliation died as well.

Even negative attachments can be grieved, when the relationship is a strong one. Louie was an aggressive, sometimes bullying sixth grader. When he died in a car accident, his teacher was surprised that one of the children most affected was Keith, a child Louie often tormented. Keith felt very guilty about the death since he often had publicly wished Louie would die or disappear. Even when the death was announced to the class, one classmate turned to Keith and loudly whispered, "I'll bet you're glad." While the attachment between the two boys was negative, it was still an attachment.

Children are attached not only to their own intimate network but to the wider world as well. Often they are caught up, as some adults are, in the lives of celebrities. Witness, for example, some of the adolescent and preadolescent magazines and posters that decorate children's bedrooms. The deaths or illnesses of rock stars, presidents, or other heroes may cause a deep sense of grief. Many adolescent youths, for example, grieved with Magic Johnson when he announced he was infected with HIV.

Another kind of unrecognized loss is an abortion. Not everyone who has an abortion experiences a grief reaction, but some do. Those who are likely to do so include those who are having an abortion for the first time, those who are ambivalent about the choice or were pressured by others to select abortion, or those who viewed the pregnancy as a solution to another problem. Adolescent girls are very likely to possess some or all of these factors that place them at risk. And, sometimes, it is not just the adolescent girl, but the boy as well, who feels a sense of loss.

One of the most common, most significant, and often unrecognized losses in adolescence is the loss of a romantic relationship, breakups of boyfriends and girlfriends. In his surveys of college freshmen, Louis LaGrand (1989) found that this was the loss cited as most significant by the largest number of respondents. Many adults, however, were unresponsive to the feelings of grief that such breakups generated.

Losses do not always have to be that of humans. From films such as *Lassie* and *National Velvet* to *Free Willy* we have celebrated the bond that children can have with animals. The loss of a pet causes a grief that parents and adults may not always appreciate. The ways that adults respond to what may be the child's first significant loss may teach children patterns that they may seek to use in subsequent deaths. For example, denying the child's grief and seeking to obtain a quick replacement may unwittingly teach the child that grief should be suppressed and that, when one faces a loss, one should seek immediate replacement. It is better to allow the child to mourn the loss and later, when he or she is ready, seek another pet. The child should be reminded that this pet, even if the same species and breed, is different than the pet that died, reinforcing the idea that each individual, and each loss, is unique.

There may be other losses, too, that children experience and grieve in childhood. The loss of childhood innocence or idealism may itself be grieved. As children grow older, they may grieve the loss of opportunity. Tom, for example, grieved deeply when he was cut from his high school varsity team. To Tom, that loss meant that he was not likely to fulfill his dream of a professional sports career.

Children experience many losses that are not due to death but are losses nonetheless. Parents, relatives, or friends divorce; friends move. People they care about may change, sometimes in the course of development, sometimes because of other factors such as drug or alcohol abuse or incarceration. Even graduations can be ambivalent experiences encompassing both pride and loss. Children and adolescents may also be placed in or removed from foster care. Foster children, foster families, and foster siblings and natural families and siblings may all be touched by loss. In all these cases, these losses may remain unrecognized by others, the child's or adolescent's grief disenfranchised.

Divorce can represent a major loss for many children. It is often complicated by the fact that children may have many ambivalent feelings about the divorce, for example, regretting the separation but being happy that any open conflict has ended. Children, too, have to mourn the loss of the one parent while simultaneously building a new relationship with that parent. They may be struggling with other feelings such as guilt and anger. And they may be struggling alone, disenfranchised by others, themselves mourning. Children can even delay their own grief, feeling that they need to support others.

Because of their ages, even children or adolescents grieving the loss of family members can be unrecognized grievers. This is particularly likely to happen to very young children. People often assume that preschool children cannot understand death and must be protected from it. When a death occurs, these children may not have an opportunity to participate in rituals, nor may their capacity to grieve even be acknowledged by others.

Developmentally or mentally impaired adolescents or children may have similar experiences. When her mother died, Jenny's family did not even notify the group home where the nineteen-year-old resided. They reasoned that, since she was mentally retarded, she would not understand what had occurred and would burden them during a difficult time. Similarly, John's parents tried to shield John, a hospitalized fourteen-year-old schizophrenic, from his brother's death.

It is true that young children or developmentally or mentally impaired adolescents may express grief differently from older children. David Crenshaw (1991) speaks of the "short sadness span" of children, the fact that they often find it intolerable to hold uncomfortably strong emotions for long periods. Their grief then may be expressed in short intensive outbursts followed by periods during which they seem unaffected by loss. But, while young children or developmentally or mentally impaired youths may grieve differently, they still grieve.

Finally, there are disenfranchising deaths. Children are not immune to shame, and certain types of deaths carry a stigma that children may hesitate to bear. Paul, an upper-class thirteen-year-old, and Maria, an impoverished fifteen-year-old, have each lost a brother to AIDS, and both are too ashamed even to acknowledge the loss to others. Their grief is similar to Jessica's, whose sister committed suicide, and to Ty's, whose father died while committing a robbery. In each case, the shame of the death has impaired the individual's ability to grieve. In each case, the grievers disenfranchised themselves. Unwilling to share their losses with peers or supportive adults, they grieve alone.

One can be disenfranchised in more than one way at once. Nineteen-year-old Jerome, for example, was doubly disenfranchised. He could not share the fact that his mother's foster children are HIV infected. He realized that disclosure not only violated the foster agency rules but would also create problems for him and his family in the neighborhood. When his young foster brother was removed and hospitalized, later to die, he did not feel free to share his grief over the loss of his first "kid brother," whom he loved deeply. But, even if he had, others might not recognize the loss of a foster brother as significant.

These examples are not meant to be exhaustive. Readers will recognize other significant losses that may be disenfranchised. Children may experience grief in a wide variety of situations and contexts that may be unrecognized by others.

Helping Children Cope with Disenfranchised Grief

Children can be assisted in dealing with disenfranchised grief in the same way that they can be helped in dealing with their loss. By respectfully listening to the child, allowing the child to share his or her feelings, adults not only provide genuine support but teach effective coping.

Adults may have to validate children's grief and to help them recognize and interpret their sense of loss. Children, too, need an opportunity to participate in grief. Quiet time, set aside to commemorate a loss, can be a powerful way to give feelings focus and recognize grief.

It takes courage to grieve. For the child, it takes courage to recognize and cope with uncomfortable feelings. For the adult, it takes courage to trust the child to do so. Yet there is little alternative. Children, as well as adults, form all sorts of attachments that are severed in all kinds of ways. When these attachments are broken, there is grief. The challenge for adults is to recognize the full scope of children's attachments and grief and to honor those feelings as best they can.

References

Crenshaw, David. 1991. *Bereavement: Counseling the Grieving throughout the Life Cycle*. New York: Continuum.

Doka, Kenneth T., ed. 1989. *Disenfranchised Grief: Coping with Hidden Sorrow*. Lexington, MA: Lexington.

King, Stephen. 1982. *The Body*. In *Different Seasons*. New York: Viking.

LaGrand, Louis. 1989. "Youth and the Disenfranchised Breakup." In *Disenfranchised Grief: Coping with Hidden Sorrow*. Lexington, MA: Lexington.

Worden, J. William. 1991. *Grief Counseling and Grief Therapy: A Handbook for the Mental Health Practitioner*. 2d ed. New York: Springer.

Talking to Children about the Terminal Illness of a Loved One

GERRI L. SWEDER

How do we prepare children when someone they love has a terminal illness? Learning to keep children engaged in the process of living becomes our fundamental challenge. Here, to help support the child during the impending death, is a series of insightful, poignant case histories.

Gerri L. Sweder, M.S.W., M.Ed., is a psychotherapist trained in working with adolescents, adults, and couples and is currently a doctoral student in clinical psychology. Her areas of concentration have been illness, loss, grief, and healing. She has taught at the preschool, high school, and graduate levels. Along with Earl A. Grollman she coauthored Teaching Your Child to Be Home Alone *(1992) and* The Working Parent Dilemma *(1986). She has appeared on numerous national radio and television programs and is a frequent speaker to educational, community, parent, and corporate organizations.*

*I worry that something is going to happen to my dad. What if he
gets sick like my mom? What will happen to me?*

—Fourteen-year-old whose mother has an inoperable
brain tumor

Terminal illness is unthinkable to children and adults alike. For everyone, it means just one thing—a move to death. Hope fades. Health de-
clines. There is the frightening spiraling downward. Control over
daily activities lessens. Terminal illness robs the patient and family of
a day's natural rhythms and leaves in its stead a world of seeming
black holes.

When told that a loved one is dying, youngsters often experience a
sense of utter helplessness and disbelief. They speak of feeling terrified,
alone, and anxious. Children may be aware yet denying at the same
time. While a loved one is struggling for physical survival, a youngster struggles to maintain some semblance of emotional balance. Each
hopes to ease the other's pain.

Children make little sense out of the notion that a parent, sibling,
grandparent, or friend is dying. They may retreat, deny, explode,
show despair, or appear to go on as if nothing has changed. Each child
chooses a different way of coping, and children's reactions will ebb and
flow. No child can sustain the inevitably intense emotions involved; to
do so would be too exhausting psychically and physically.

The child's age and maturity will affect his or her response to the
horrific news. Infants and toddlers with little or no spoken vocabulary
have few words available to express feeling a sense of disequilibrium
and limited ability to comprehend what is spoken to them. Sensitive
to family tension, these little people will react when serious illness presents itself. They show their stress by being fussier or withdrawing.
As a result of emotional upheaval, they might be unable to soothe
themselves or be comforted by others. If changes in feeding, sleep, and
play schedules occur because a parent is distracted or distraught, there
can be consequences. Infants and toddlers need to experience their
world as a safe and trusting place, but terminal illness disrupts this at-

mosphere. There can be psychological effects when early attachments are disturbed. Procuring reliable and nurturing substitute care is essential to ensure stability.

Preschool Children

By preschool age, children have some sense of personal individuality. This generally enables them to tolerate and accept circumscribed separation from parents. For them, life is lived in the moment. They engage others in verbal interaction and rejoice in activities with peers. Thoughts move from one idea to another without apparent connection. There is a blurring of the real and the imagined. Games include "playing dead," but they cannot grasp fully what it means to die. Adults may note that preschoolers offer comfort and consolation to the ill and grieving, but only fleetingly. They cannot comprehend the magnitude of death or its permanence.

Although impulsive, these young children crave consistency. Changes in caregivers or routines should be carefully thought out and regular schedules maintained as far as is possible. The child should be allowed to spend time with the dying loved one. While able, the ill parent should continue to care for the child. The dying patient needs to feel involved and valued; the preschooler needs the love, companionship, and warmth of the ill parent.

At this age, children often believe that something they did or said caused the sickness, although they may not let on to others that they feel this way. They require repeated reassurances that an argument with mom or refusing to kiss grandpa good-bye did not induce the illness.

Brief explanations are most appropriate. Stating, "Mommy is very sick," is important. Honesty is necessary, and simplicity is just as valuable. On the other hand, youngsters should not be overloaded, given more information than they can handle. Reporting, "Mommy has chemotherapy three days a week to help her get better," is too detailed; better to tell them, "Mommy is taking medicine so she won't feel so bad," which responds to one of the child's basic fears—Mommy in pain.

The absence of one or both parents for a period of time, for instance, during a hospital stay, may cause a youngster to regress. Bed-wetting, thumb-sucking, and nightmares can be expressions of emotional stress and grief. The child will experience losses before death arrives. These cries for help must be met with reassurance and understanding. Relatives, siblings, and family friends are best suited to offer comfort during times of particular distress.

Latency: Ages Six to Ten

Beginning around age six, the youngster moves into a wider world. Demands for performance and adaptation to new roles are placed on the child by school, parents, society, and peers. Youngsters develop multiple connections, and for the first time they feel that they are establishing identities other than simply daughter or son.

As they spend more time socializing, children learn to make comparisons between their household and others. They become aware that not all homes have a dying loved one. Youngsters may be jealous that friends' families are not rocked by emotional turmoil. They long for a normal home life; they might find creative reasons to stay away.

Often hurting children need encouragement to maintain activities in school, sports, and religious education and with friends. Adults help ease youngsters' guilt about being away by acknowledging the pain, sorrow, and unease that many feel when around a dying relative. Finding ways to include the child in caretaking allows the youngster to feel useful, valued, and less afraid. Establishing a routine helps children know what is expected. One child brought his father his medicine before dinner. Another read a story to his terminally ill sibling at bedtime. Keeping the connection while a loved one deteriorates will be a challenge.

Nine-year-old Paul suddenly began avoiding entering his father's room. He believed that his dad no longer knew him. This boy adored his father and was deeply troubled by his conflicting emotions of love and dread. Giving voice to his fears decreased his sense of isolation. Paul's grandfather started to accompany him to his father's bedside, helping reengage Paul in daily conversations. Even as death neared, Paul felt less alone and scared. Those visits became treasured memories after Paul's father died. During the final phase of his father's illness, Paul's family engaged the services of a psychotherapist. As an only child, Paul had no siblings to share his terrible loss. The therapist's office became a safe place to talk, play, and show anger and sadness.

During the latency period, youngsters become capable of concrete thought. They now have a more durable sense of the past, present, and future. They are increasingly inquisitive about what is happening around them. By age eight or nine, youngsters confronted with terminal illness will ask for specific information. They will be curious about the causes of the sickness: How did my sister get cystic fibrosis? Will I get ill and die too? How do you know I won't? Their concerns will focus on outcomes: What if the medicine doesn't work? What if the operation doesn't make Daddy better? Posing questions does not imply an emotional or intellectual ability to accept the responses. Talking with children at this age requires an acute sensitivity to what the child wants to know—and where the child should be protected. Because youngsters now have well-developed language skills, adults may assume that they are capable of assimilating the many details that surround illness. They cannot. Although truth should be a guiding principle, truth can be delivered in many forms. Responding in a gentle, respectful, and discreet manner is best.

A Case History: Being Involved

Michael G. was ten years old (the younger of two children) when his father was diagnosed with cancer. One year later Mr. G. was dead. Michael's father, Larry, was a loving man, a successful executive, and a community activist when he was stricken. Although overcome with grief and bewilderment, Mrs. G. included Michael in the living and dying of his father from the time the cancer was diagnosed:

> Larry wasn't feeling well. He complained of backaches. That wasn't like him since he was in excellent shape. We went to several doctors before one told us the news. We were devastated. I could hardly hear what was

said. I remember shaking. I didn't know how I was going to tell the boys. But I knew I had to talk to them right away. I didn't want them hearing the news from anyone else.

Larry and I decided we would talk to the boys together. We told them that Daddy has cancer and that is going to make him very sick. We explained that he is going to have treatments, take medicine, and that he'll probably lose his hair and a lot of weight. But that he would still be the same father who loves them.

A few days later Michael asked me if Larry was going to die. I told him we weren't sure, but it was certainly possible.

Larry didn't respond well to chemotherapy. He'd be in bed for days looking pale and unable to eat. Michael was great. He'd bring his homework into our room just to be near Larry. It was wonderful for both of them. No matter what was happening I always wanted the boys to feel included. A few times they went to the oncologist with us. They had their own questions to ask. We didn't want it to seem mysterious. It was scary enough.

Larry tried to make it to Michael's softball games. He had been the coach, and it was so hard for both of them when he had to give it up. Being there made Larry feel a part of what was happening, and Michael didn't have to feel that cancer was taking everything away.

I kept his teacher informed of what was going on at home, and she called whenever she noticed anything I should be aware of. The school was quite supportive. There were many days Michael would leave class to go and talk with the guidance counselor.

Michael was aware of things changing. As Larry became weaker we hired a male nurse. We wanted Larry to be able to come downstairs for as long as he could to be with us. He'd usually be sleeping in the family room when Michael came home from school. Michael always came in the door quietly, afraid to disturb his father. Michael worshiped his father. It was terrible for him to see Larry slipping away.

It was painful for the boys to see Larry suffer. He wanted to live so. He had done all the right things, exercised, eaten healthy foods, had a loving family. Now he was dying a wretched death. It was horrid. But we were going to function as best we could. Michael continued with sports and did pretty well in school. His friends came to our house because he didn't want to be away from his dad for too long.

When Larry became weaker still, we all knew he would soon be dead.

Near the end Michael and his brother ate dinner and slept in our room. They didn't want to be alone. It was good for Larry to have them near. Before he died, he spent time with the two of them, talking and crying.

This ten-year-old was given the opportunity to grieve. He was included in the family dialogue from the time of diagnosis until his father's death. Questions were answered, feelings respected. Maintaining contact was encouraged and supported. Flexible eating and sleeping arrangements were created that met this family's needs.

Adolescence

By adolescence, children have the ability to move beyond the self, to form hypotheses about the world, and to search for life's deeper meanings. They have a heightened body consciousness. Independence is prized. Because terminal illness is marked by physical deterioration and increasing dependency, adolescents are even more aware of the terrible loss and need the opportunity to express the grief.

A loved one's terminal illness comes at that point of development when adolescents are learning to establish what Erikson refers to as "ego identity." They are becoming more fully integrated people with distinct likes and dislikes. They seek independence from home and interdependence with peers. A basic core of values that has been evolving over time is solidified. Relationships take on deeper and more intense meanings. Adolescence is also a time of upheaval, of renegotiating what it is to be part of a family, a community, a society. Adolescents are holding on at the same time that they are separating. For parents, this sense of uncertainty and disruption can be wrenching. For the family with a terminally ill member, letting go can become even more complicated.

Adolescents may need permission to move on when the pressure to stay and take care of everyone may be great. For those of high school age, growth involves continuing a social life, keeping up with schoolwork, and participating in extracurricular activities as well as adhering to family rules. The adolescent should not feel that the house has become "off limits." A sense of secrecy and shame can be created when access to the home is limited. Besides, the terminally ill parent or sibling may still enjoy the sights and sounds that are unique to the teenage years. Peers can provide a supportive network for the adolescent who is grieving an impending loss.

Not everyone experiences a sense of closeness with friends when there is a terminal illness. Some adolescents feel profoundly alone, even in the company of others. Talk of upcoming exams, planning for the weekend, or just general chatter appears banal. An internal dialogue grips many youngsters as they find themselves living in different worlds. At school life appears whole, while at home everything seems shattered. Adolescents who are able to speak to someone—a family friend or relative, a school counselor, a member of the clergy, or a therapist—about these "crazy" feelings often express relief at being able to unburden themselves.

Not all homes welcome outsiders. Some families guard their privacy more than others. Many restrict access to the family circle as death nears. Such reactions must be respected. The energy needed to take care of and comfort a dying loved one leaves few resources for anything or anyone else. Families need to attend to adolescents' vulnerability to rejection at this time and find ways to ensure their inclusion in the terminally ill person's life up to and past the time of death. Driving to a doctor's appointment or chemotherapy helps some feel that they are doing something. Renting videos to watch together or just being near one another feels comforting for others. If hospice services are utilized, prepare teenagers for the presence of caring strangers who may seem to them like intruders. Help them understand that hospice is a supplement to the family, not a replacement.

Secrecy: A Case History

Sixteen-year-old Beth L. first began noticing changes with her father before she was told of his illness. She weeps as she recalls her father's illness:

> My father stopped driving at the end of September, and then I noticed he wasn't going to work every day. That was all very unusual for him. He loved his work and would never be out. He wouldn't finish dinner

and would leave the table. I thought he seemed lazy or was exaggerating his being sick. I didn't understand what was wrong. Nobody said anything, and I was too scared to ask. By the middle of October my dad wasn't driving at all, and he was hardly able to go to work. It was then that my mother told me that my father had something that was very rare but that the tests showed he should be okay. My mom said he had a tumor, but it was never defined. The whole time I kept thinking he was going to get better.

He started radiation in November, and soon he lost his hair. He had to stay in the hospital for two weeks that first time. I think it was better for us when he was in the hospital because we didn't have to see it daily. I remember when I would visit. He didn't look like a man. He was just so skinny and bald and lying there. It smelled when we went in. By January you could tell that nothing was working. I would find myself crying in school. It just came in spurts. I'd cry myself to sleep at night. I don't ever remember seeing my mother cry. I don't think she liked it when I cried. It upset her even more.

I asked my mother if my dad would die. She said he could, but she never said he was going to die. I never thought he would die because no one said he would.

I didn't like having people over. I was embarrassed. Once I had this friend over, and when she saw my dad, I could tell she was surprised. He didn't have his wig on, and I yelled at him after and said how could you forget to wear the wig. I yelled at my own father! I felt so bad because it was so hard for him to wear a wig.

I spent most of that winter inside my house. Those five months went so slowly and so quickly. All of a sudden he wasn't there. I don't think I dealt with it very much. I don't talk about it to many people.

The five months he was sick were the worst. Friends were of no help. I would get upset if people did ask about him. I'd get upset if they didn't ask. I wanted people to treat me nicer than they did. But I know that when one of my friend's parents died I didn't know what to say to her. This was before my dad was sick. Now I'd know to keep calling.

Days before he died I couldn't go to school. I'd go to class, then I'd call my mother and tell her I had to go to the hospital. I didn't want to leave my father.

I remember the day he died. He slipped in and out of a coma. At 11:00 that morning he didn't seem to know us anymore. He didn't even seem like my dad. He was only eighty pounds. He was hardly there. This priest from the hospital came by to be with us. He said your dad is going to die. That wasn't very comforting. I remember watching my grand-parents and thinking how hard it was for them to watch their son die. He died at 2:00. They pulled a curtain around him, and I went back to give him a hug. I didn't want to leave. I still can't believe it. If I only knew what was happening, I would have been nicer to him.

Beth suffered on her own. With little clear information, she was left to guess what was happening to her father. Not having been given a realistic appraisal of her father's condition, Beth experienced conflict-ing emotions and received little support. The frightening and rapid changes in her father's condition became a source of confusion and alarm. The long hospital stays increased the tension and sense of isola-tion. Beth's mother was too absorbed in her own sorrow to be able to offer much support to her children. Being a quiet person by nature, she closed down. She did not intend to cut off her daughters, but she was overwhelmed and not able to admit to herself the serious nature of the illness. In the end, it was Beth who initiated being with her dad, by asking to leave school. Sitting at his bedside in the hospital became the most comfortable place to be. This father and daughter found a way of saying good-bye by being together. Sadly, they endured months of separate agony before reaching this point. A shroud of secrecy devel-oped when adults were afraid or unsure of what to say or how truthful to be. Early recognition of the serious nature of the illness might have prevented much of the guessing and uncertainty that dominated Beth's thinking. There may have been less embarrassment and more sympa-thy expressed had there been more understanding of the disease's course.

It is understandable and laudable for parents to want to protect their children from pain. Youngsters do need responsible adults to filter the information with which they are supplied. Taking cues from a child can help establish how much is too much. Move slowly and thought-fully. When parents emotionally retreat or withhold information, they lay the groundwork for emotional upheaval.

The atmosphere of the household is the vital force influencing the way in which family members cope with crisis. Families who are able to articulate feelings and support one another can provide succor and safety for a child. (During critical times the definition of *family* may expand to include those residing in the home and other close relatives and friends who are committed and available to provide emotional sustenance.) When speaking about the unspeakable is too painful or overwhelming or not part of the family pattern, outside intervention can prove invaluable. Marked changes in behavior such as acting out or withdrawing, sleep or eating disturbances, or frequent stomachaches or headaches are signs of emotional turmoil that may also indicate the need for professional consultation. Sometimes being out of the stressful environment allows a youngster to voice fears and concerns that have been trapped inside. Clergy, school counselors, or psychotherapists trained in family and/or grief work are skilled at sustaining discussions with children and with other family members. Recognizing that going for help is a sign of courage and strength is a crucial first step.

Not having someone to hear your cry can have lasting implications. Such is the case of Suzanne K., the second youngest of five, whose mother died at age forty-three of a brain tumor. Suzanne was thirteen. Only one younger sibling lived at home:

> I have no happy or warm thoughts of my childhood. I don't remember my house as one filled with laughter. It's scary I don't remember the good times. I was left out of a lot of the conversations. I was left on my own a lot. I knew I had to behave, so I didn't bring friends over to the house. My mother couldn't handle it. She was sick for most of my childhood. I feel sad about it. I don't remember any great time with her or special conversations. We were never close. She was a kind, giving person, but she couldn't do much with me. When she got bad, she couldn't take care of us at all. My father was a kind person also, but he didn't show any emotion or affection. Neither of my parents were demonstrative. What I didn't get from my mom I also didn't get from my dad. I knew they loved me, but there was no showing it in my house.
>
> There was a mystery in our family as to what was wrong with my mom. She had high blood pressure and always had to watch her diet. I remember her being tired a lot and taking naps in the middle of the day. She'd get angry with us pretty easily. My memories of her are when she wasn't in good health. She began getting dizzy spells and falling down. That's when she went for tests. She'd be gone for a while, then come

home. She never got any better. I just remember her going back and forth to the hospital. My older sister talked to me most about what was happening with my mother.

I envied kids who had parents who were healthy. My mother always looked sick, and she didn't take good care of herself. I used to want to comb her hair differently or tell her what to wear, but I never did.

After my mother died, my biggest fear was that I was going to walk into a room and see my father dead. I thought he was so old. He was a lot older than my mother. I lived with that fear for the next five years. I couldn't tell anyone. I just know that image stayed with me that one day I'd find him dead. I kept thinking that I would be the one to discover him, too. It was pretty scary.

In this household, Suzanne missed an important part of her childhood and of herself. She speaks poignantly of not knowing her mother. There were few "special conversations" to hold onto growing up. Little opportunity was offered to share daily experiences, friends made and lost, goings-on in school, changes within her body. There was no place to share moments of joy or sadness. Suzanne did not feel touched by the sweetness of being nurtured. She hardly knew that exquisite sense of being enveloped by a warm and loving motherly presence.

Illness came between Suzanne and her mother. Feeling incapacitated by her illness, Suzanne's mother was less able to participate in her daughter's upbringing.

Home was a refuge to the mother but oppressive to the daughter. There were many prohibitions: don't speak in a loud tone of voice, don't invite friends over, don't go near mother, don't get anyone upset. What appeared to be the consequences of not following these proscriptions? Mother will become sicker.

Suzanne was left with a sense of trepidation. She observed her mother's sleeping more, increased headaches, and need for little noise. Days were spent in a darkened bedroom with the door closed. Silence permeated the household.

No one ever sat down with this anxious thirteen-year-old to ask how she was doing, to answer questions, or to prepare her for her mother's death. There was no closure for mother or daughter. They inhabited the same space, but there was an invisible barrier keeping them apart. Illness sucked up much of the air, leaving this family choking with fear.

When the end came, Suzanne remembers, "It was such a shock when she died. I couldn't talk about it to anyone. I didn't know how I felt. I just couldn't believe it. Even though I knew she was sick I could never imagine my mother dying." Being unprepared for this ultimate loss, Suzanne retreated. Grief for her was private.

A terminal illness took more than a mother's life. A relationship also died, one that never had time to develop. Few words were shared about the extraordinary transition into puberty. Advice about school and boys was garnered elsewhere. A childhood was marked by having to feel invisible. Normal activities were curtailed. Friends could not visit. Loud sounds were taboo. And there was the sense of embarrassment painfully spoken. What does it feel like to have a parent look different than other mothers—to look sick when others appear robust? For those who strive to be like peers, anything that separates can be hurtful and confusing. Unable to affect change creates a sense of powerlessness. Suzanne felt disconnected from her mother, her family, her peers, even herself. The feeling of isolation that she experienced seemed pervasive. Therapeutic intervention by a school counselor or trained psychotherapist might have been able to release some of the sadness, fear, anger, and bewilderment that this girl suffered in silence.

What do all children have in common when a loved one is terminally ill? They need a gentle honesty, information appropriate to their age and developmental level, the ability to grieve in their own way, loving, supportive adults, someone to listen no matter the hour, respect for their feelings, limits on behavior, consistency as much as is possible, and time to be a child.

Chapter Five

Toward Siblings' Understanding and Perspectives of Death

BETTY DAVIES

Siblings usually receive little attention when a brother or sister dies. They are asked, "How is your mother or father?" Even though they may experience a wrenching loss, few family members or friends ask, "How are you today?" How can we reinforce their sense of personal worth and with open communication help them grieve in their own way when their sister or brother dies?

Betty Davies, R.N., Ph.D., is professor, School of Nursing, University of British Columbia, Vancouver, Canada, and investigator, Research Division, British Columbia's Children's Hospital. Davies is the first nurse, and the first psychosocial researcher, to be awarded an investigatorship, the only one of its kind in Canada. She is a founding member of the board of HUGS Children's Hospice Society, whose major work is the establishment of Canuck Place, the first free-standing hospice in North America devoted only to children. She is director of the Bereavement Program as well as chair of the Hospice Care Committee. Her seminal work pertaining to bereavement in siblings forms the basis for many presentations and publications.

Following the death of a child, the agony within a family is pervasive and profound. For parents, a child's death represents the loss of their hopes, their dreams, their future; they are faced with emotions so intense as to be debilitating. For surviving children, the death of a sibling means the loss of a playmate, a confidante, a rival, a role model, a friend. But, in the case of sibling loss, the child's experience may be further complicated by the failure of those around him or her even to acknowledge that he or she has suffered a significant loss.

Just as their parents grieve for the loss of a child, so do children grieve for the loss of a sibling. But, as we have learned, children express their grief differently than adults. Children cannot relate to the past and the future; they cannot anticipate, prepare, compare, place in perspective, analyze, explain, and draw conclusions as adults can. Adults have more ways of coping with raw emotion, more ways of drawing back and making it the object of their attention. Grieving parents, however, may be emotionally unavailable to their surviving children, and the loss for the surviving children can double. They not only lose a brother or sister but also, in a sense, their parents as well.

Sibling Relationships

Most children have at least one sibling with whom they will spend more time during their lives than with any other person. Moreover, children spend more time together than with any other family members and exert a powerful influence in shaping one another's identity.

Even before the actual birth of a new baby into the family, a special bond forms between the children. The older child anticipates becoming the "big" brother or sister; he or she learns early how to help care for the new "baby." As time goes on, siblings play and explore the world together, teach and coach one another, alternatively fight with and defend one another, confide in and share secrets with one another.

Seldom, however, are the relationships between siblings simple. Even when two siblings are friends, their relationship will pass through stressful times. The competitiveness of human nature seems to mandate that the sibling relationship is not always rosy. Heated conversations often include exclamations like, "Get out of my room, and don't you ever show your face in here again!" In childhood, it is natural for children to fight with one another, to shout and scream, and to blame one another. It is part of growing up in a family and learning how to channel strong emotions.

But none of the experiences that siblings have with one another prepares them for the death of a brother or sister. The emotions experienced by siblings are rooted in their relationships with each other, and the death of one may reactivate rivalries, guilt, and resentment among the others as well as the anger, sadness, and sorrow of grief. The emotional closeness that existed between siblings prior to the death of one of the children tends to be related to the outcome of the surviving child's grieving process (Davies 1988b). The closer the relationship was before death, the more behavior problems the surviving siblings demonstrate afterward. There is no doubt that, when a sibling dies, an emptiness remains in the lives of the surviving children that no one else can fill.

Influencing Factors

Faulty Assumptions about Siblings' Grief

Many conditions affect a child's reactions to the loss of a sibling. Sometimes, adults do not adequately understand that children follow a maturational process that allows them to comprehend death in different ways at different developmental levels, assuming that children need to know more or less than they actually do. In some cases, parents and other adults assume that the children will not experience the same degree of grief as they themselves are feeling, and they ignore the siblings' responses. In other cases, parents and other adults assume that children cannot cope with the death and will try to protect them from the pain, excluding them from conversations or from participating in events such as the funeral. Such assumptions mean that siblings are often the most neglected family members when a child dies.

Parents' Reactions

After the death of a child, most parents can barely function, let alone look after the needs of their other children. It is not that they are unconcerned about the surviving children; their capacity is just sorely limited because they are overwhelmed by their own grief. Since parents are the most influential role models for their children, the surviving children are also placed at a disadvantage because of the devastating effects of the death on their parents.

The children's grief may be compounded by seeing their parents' distress and vulnerability. As one bereaved sibling recalled, "To have to accept my brother's death and my father's humanity all in the same day was a big order" (LaTour 1983, 36). Children may be frightened by the explosive nature of their parents' feelings. Children try to understand the reason for Daddy's being so angry and often attribute his outbursts to something they have done. Siblings also don't realize how long grief lasts, so they become impatient with their parents' ongoing grief. Siblings want their parents to be "normal" again. Confused by their parents' reactions and wanting to make things "right" again, children often suppress their own feelings and questions. But, whether children are suppressing or expressing their feelings, they are nevertheless grieving and are affected by their parents' expression of their own sorrow.

Family Reactions

Whereas adults seek and are usually given prompt and detailed information about the death and related events, in most cases children, especially younger ones, are entirely dependent on their parents for information and support. Furthermore, if adults wish to find additional understanding and comfort, they can do so; children can seldom turn elsewhere if family members are unsympathetic to their needs. Unfortunately, after a child's death, just when surviving siblings most need the stability and security of their family, the family may be the least able to help.

After any death, the family itself must restructure and readjust; doing so after the death of a child is exceedingly difficult. How families manage this process of adaptation is greatly influenced by the degree of cohesiveness in the family and by the amount of support the family receives from extended family members and friends. These same conditions affect how surviving siblings adapt to the loss. When siblings experience closeness or a sense of togetherness in their family, and when they too share in the support offered by friends and other family members, they demonstrate fewer behavior problems following the death (Davies 1988a). Special links that may exist between children and other family members, particularly grandparents, can be especially significant in helping the siblings cope with their grief.

Sibling Responses

Immediate Responses

The responses of children to the death of a sibling may be as varied as the children themselves. Adults therefore need to be prepared for each child to react in his or her own way and not to judge any response as "good" or "bad."

Right from the time they are told about the death, children may respond in ways for which adults are totally unprepared. Younger children interrupt the conversation to ask if they can go and play. Sometimes older children just leave the room, wanting to be on their own. These reactions may be difficult for parents and other adults to understand if they do not realize that these are normal responses for children. Such behavior does not mean that the child didn't "love" her sister or that she took the news "well." Children, like adults, resort to familiar patterns when they hear bad news or are anxious or afraid. For children, playing is familiar. To return to play, or to escape into solitude, is an attempt to seek some control over a situation that seems so far beyond their control.

In response to the death, children experience many of the same reactions that adults do, but these reactions are expressed in different ways. After the death of a sibling, and for up to three years afterward, children have been reported to have had frequent headaches, stomachaches, and other aches and pains and to have had sleeping difficulties such as not wanting to go to bed, wanting to sleep with the light on, being afraid of the dark, waking up frequently, or having bad dreams. Some children have trouble eating, either eating too much or eating too little. Others are anxious about being alone or about trying out new activities; they may have difficulty concentrating in school or remembering. They may be sad and withdrawn; they may act out. They are frequently lonely (Davies 1988a; McCown 1987; McCown and Davies 1993). Many of the immediate responses diminish over time, but others continue indefinitely for some children.

Ongoing Responses

Asking questions. Children want information and want to participate in the grief process. They want to know what has happened to their brother or sister. Their questions may continue for weeks, months, even years. With each new stage of cognitive development, children ask questions from their newly learned perspectives. Most often, they ask questions that are difficult to answer: "Why did the baby die?" "Why didn't you stop the doctor from taking Johnny away?" "Suzie will come back for my birthday party, won't she?" Older children will want to know how the deceased child can breathe in the ground or what happens to the body. As siblings enter the teen years, they may want to review the exact details of what happened.

Asking questions is also a way of seeking reassurance that they or their parents will not die too. For parents, such questions stimulate new waves of grief, yet it is important not to scold children for their questions. In such cases, children begin to think that the situation is even too awful to talk about. Then, instead of being verbalized, the questions gnaw away as worrisome concerns in the silence of the child's own mind.

Answering children's questions about their deceased sibling is often acutely painful for parents. Some parents may be simply unable to help their surviving children during the first weeks, or even months, after the death. In such cases, it may be helpful to identify another adult for the child to talk to, a grandparent, an aunt, a close family friend, someone with whom the child has established a good rapport. Ask this person to be the child's companion for a while, reassuring the child that Mom and Dad still love her but that this person is someone to whom she can go when her parents seem just too overwhelmed.

Trying to explain what happened in religious terms is often confusing to younger children. It is better to say that we do not know why the child died, that we don't always understand the ways of God, than to say, for example, that Johnny went to heaven because he was such a good little boy that God wanted him for a special angel. Siblings tend to interpret such explanations in two self-destructive ways: they compare themselves to the "good" child, concluding that they are not as good, an interpretation that lowers their self-esteem; or they decide that being good means being taken away, so they resolve not to be good, and, while their resultant misbehavior may get them into trouble, at least it allows them to remain with their parents.

Siblings want to take part in events that occur after the death. Children who were more involved in the rituals following their sibling's death had fewer behavior problems up to three years following the death (Davies 1988a, 1988b). To isolate siblings from these events, for whatever reason, is very frightening for them and may create additional problems. In studies of the long-term effects of sibling grief, many siblings recalled that they did not know what was happening at the time of the death (Davies 1990; Rosen 1986). They felt left out, lonely, and confused about not having their questions answered. And many carried with them concerns about what had happened, even decades later. Unless children are given some factual basis, like being told the story, seeing the body, or attending the funeral, they may think that their brother or sister is not really dead. Children's choices, however, must be respected. No child should be forced to see the body, attend the funeral, or visit the cemetery. Some siblings have reported not wanting to go to the cemetery but doing so for the sake of their parents, who are unhappy if they do not.

Soon after the death, children are concerned about the structure of their lives. They may want to know what will happen to Johnny's room, who will take out the garbage now, who will walk the dog. Their concerns may seem mundane to grieving adults, but to the child they are significant, reflecting a need to be reassured that life will go on as usual. To siblings, it seems like everything has changed, so to continue as much as possible with the routines that give stability to children's lives is critical.

When a child dies after a long-term illness, the likelihood is increased that the other children have been prepared for the death. But this is not always so. Children are very adaptable, and they often come to believe that their ill brother or sister will continue to live as he or she has done for so long (Brett and Davies 1988). Moreover, children may not have been actively involved with the changes associated with the ill child's deteriorating condition and may not have been present at the death, especially if it occurred in the hospital. In such cases, the siblings are confronted with a "sudden" death, and their responses may be more like those of children whose sibling dies unexpectedly. In other families, the siblings have been actively involved in the care of the ill child and have participated in the events leading to the death. Such involvement before the death usually means that the child has been somewhat prepared for it. However, no amount of preparation can prepare anyone for the actual death of a loved one. Siblings too will still feel the loss acutely after the death of the ill child.

Feeling guilty. Children can feel very responsible for the death of their brother or sister. In one study, about 50 percent of the twenty-three siblings interviewed reported feeling guilty about their sibling's death (Rosen 1986). Older children, like their parents, have a sense of being responsible for younger children. They ask the unanswerable questions, "What if . . . ," and "If only. . . ." Other children feel guilty just for being alive, for having wished their sibling dead, or for feeling jealous over their parents' grief for the deceased sibling. Younger children feel guilty or somehow responsible for the death because of their exaggerated sense of omnipotence, assuming that the world revolves around them. They remember having yelled at their sibling, having hit him, or having thrown the baby's toy out of reach, thereby, in their minds, causing the death.

Feelings of responsibility for the death are not limited to cases of sudden or accidental death. For example, one child with cancer died after a serious episode with chicken pox. The surviving child felt responsible for his brother's death because he knew of a child at a nearby school with chicken pox and felt that he must have brought the virus home, even though he had not had any contact with the infected child. Parents need to reassure their surviving children again and again that they were in no way responsible for the death. It may seem strange to do so, especially when it seems like there is no rational reason for the child's feelings of guilt, but it may be all that is necessary to ease the child's mind. Some parents may be afraid that mentioning such things will only "put ideas in the child's head," but giving siblings such reassurances is necessary even when the child does not talk about having such feelings.

Guilty feelings may stem from siblings' feelings that they should have died instead of their brother or sister. The child who died was special in some way—he was the smartest one, or the most athletic, or the one who made everyone laugh—and the one who remains feels that she is "not enough" to make her parents happy now. Such feelings may be reinforced by parents who eulogize their deceased child, often extolling his virtues without mentioning his shortcomings. Surviving children may feel as though they simply cannot compare to the child who died and wish that they had died instead. They may resent the deceased child, which can also lead to guilt, or, as some siblings have done, they may suffer from continuing low self-esteem (Martinson, Davies, and McClowry 1987).

Feelings of not being enough are sometimes inadvertently reinforced by parents, for example, by displaying pictures only of the deceased child, without any pictures of the surviving children anywhere to be seen. It is important for parents to keep alive the memories of their deceased child, but the degree to which this is done has implications for the surviving children (Davies 1987). Surviving children need to be included in the parents' discussion about the deceased child if they are to benefit from the constant mention of the child's name: "I got so tired of hearing my mom talk about my sister. It was like I had disappeared. . . . She never talked about me, and I am still alive. . . . Doesn't she care about me anymore?" On the other hand, giving the surviving child the message that he is all that the parents have left places a different burden on the child. Such messages reinforce the child's sense of responsibility for the parents' well-being. It is not unusual for surviving children to assume the role of parent, wanting to alleviate their parents' pain and sadness. Such children often feel a need to make up somehow to their parents for their loss of a child.

Some parents admit to having the perplexing feelings that the child who died was, in fact, their favorite child. It is important that parents acknowledge such feelings, but not to the surviving children. This is an issue to be shared with a counselor, someone who can help the parent with such difficult feelings. To discuss such issues with the other children only makes them feel even worse.

Parents must not assume that their remaining children know that they too are special and that the death of one child has not diminished their value. Children must be told, again and again, that they are special to their parents.

School-related problems. School plays an important role in the lives of older children. At the time of the death, parents should call the school to inform the principal and the child's teacher about what has happened. The adults should be told the facts surrounding the death so that they can dispel any rumors that might be circulating. They should also be informed of any particular problems that the child is having. Parents and teachers should keep in mind that some children may need time away from school altogether in order to deal with their grief.

Inability to concentrate is one of the most common school-related problems experienced by grieving siblings. Teachers need to be aware of such difficulties and be patient with and understanding of the needs of bereaved children. Teachers must guard against giving the child too much sympathy or against avoiding the child entirely. They may become impatient when children prefer to stay by themselves or are reluctant to participate. Often a surviving sibling may not wish to speak up in class or may withdraw from group activities. Some surviving siblings of young adolescent age may feel "different" from their peers and withdraw from interaction at a time when socializing with peers is necessary for completion of the tasks of this age group (Davies 1991). Teachers are in a position to notice such behavior and to spend time with these children or refer them to the school counselor or to an individual who specializes in helping children manage their grief.

After the death of a sibling, some children become very engrossed in their schoolwork. They strive for perfection in all that they do and struggle to achieve as much as they can. These children are often the ones who receive little attention for their grief because their behavior is perceived as commendable. Parents and teachers need to note such behavior as well, to determine whether the motivation for the diligent behavior lies in feelings of inadequacy that push the child to prove his or her worth through achievement.

Dealing with peers at school may sometimes be a problem for bereaved siblings. Out of their own discomfort and lack of understanding, other children can say cruel and thoughtless things. On her first day aboard the school bus after her sister's death, one child was greeted by another child's taunting voice singing, "Mary, Mary went to bed, and couldn't get up in the morning." *Mary* was the name of the deceased sister, who had died suddenly in her sleep from a brain aneurysm.

Frightening thoughts. Surviving children may be confronted with a variety of frightening thoughts following the death of a sibling. Being left alone is one of the most common fears. Such thoughts may stem from the fear that they, or their parents, might also die. Siblings who are left as only children as a result of a sibling's death are aware that, should their parents die, they would be all alone. Younger children respond by clinging to their parents, not wanting to leave them, not wanting to go to bed, or not sleeping when their parents are away from them. Older children may stay close to home, feeling anxious about encountering new experiences. Other children may stay away from home for fear of upsetting their parents or of adding to their parents' sadness. This is particularly true for children who perceive that they are somehow a painful reminder to their parents of the child who died.

In some instances, siblings' fears of venturing out may be reinforced by parents' overprotectiveness of their surviving children. Parents, fearful of losing another child, may hesitate to allow them to resume everyday activities. In this case, siblings are either kept close to home or sent off with dire warnings that reinforce their fears. The tensions that result from such fears are particularly difficult for families with teenagers. Freedom is a major developmental issue for adolescents, and it seems impossible for parents who have lost a child to allow even a portion of the freedom their teenagers would like, especially if their child has died traumatically. Explaining the basis for their reaction, while reaffirming their love for the child, can be helpful: "Please call me if you will be later than you have said. When you don't call, I panic because of what happened to your brother. I know this is irrational, but I want you to understand how it is for me and to know how much I love you."

Not talking. One of the most frequent concerns expressed by the parents of bereaved siblings is that their children do not talk; as a result, the parents do not know what is going on with them. Many bereaved siblings themselves admit to not talking, especially to their parents because they don't want to upset them. In studies of adults who recall the experience of losing a sibling in childhood, most of them indicate that they did not talk to anyone about their sibling's death (Davies 1990, 1991; Rosen 1986). Feelings of wanting to protect their parents are sometimes strengthened by well-meaning adults who tell the children that they should be good, or not be sad, or not cry, or not mention the name of the deceased child, so as not to upset their parents. It may help if siblings can talk with someone other than their parents, someone they trust and can converse with easily, and if parents understand that their children can benefit from talking to others.

Parents and other adults can encourage surviving children to express their grief by setting an example themselves. By expressing their own sadness and anger, by sharing their tears, parents assist the siblings in understanding their parents' grief and offer the siblings a lesson in learning that grief can be shared and dealt with openly.

Talking too much about the deceased sibling can, however, be problematic. Some parents, for example, mention the deceased child at every subsequent major family event. Their references may be intended to be helpful, such as the comment made by a father to his surviving daughter on her graduation from high school: "Your sister would be so happy to see you graduate today." But such comments, particularly if they are frequent, instill in surviving children a sense of not being important enough to have their "own" day. The graduating daughter, for example, explained, "Just for once, I wish Dad would forget about my sister." On the special occasions for living children, it is a good idea for parents to mention their deceased child only if the surviving child mentions the child first. This is not to say that parents must forget their deceased children but rather that parents focus on the needs of the living children on their special days. As time goes on, it is also important that parents and children together decide how to handle special days, such as holidays and anniversaries.

Sometimes, parents and surviving children will share their memories of the deceased child in ways that are helpful for all members of the family, for example, recalling special things about the child. It is best if they can do this as a family, perhaps while engaged in an activity, for example, sorting through the child's belongings. It is also helpful for parents to ask their other children if they would like to have anything that belonged to their deceased sibling to keep for themselves. What the children choose to do with the belonging that they have selected is their decision. They may put it away or keep it on display, but they will have it to remember for as long as they choose.

Growth Out of Pain

For many siblings, the death of a brother or a sister has not only problematic outcomes but some growth-promoting effects as well (Davies 1990, 1991). Looking back, many siblings perceived some positive outcomes of the experience. They felt more comfortable with death and were able to help, instead of avoid, other individuals who were facing a death in the family. They felt that their experience facilitated the development of a sensitive outlook on life, and they generally felt good about what they had learned. As occurs with any traumatic experience, there is the potential for growth as a positive outcome of the death of a sibling. That positive outcome can be enhanced when parents and other adults realize that surviving children suffer a unique loss when a brother or sister dies.

References

Brett, K., and B. Davies. 1988. "What Does It Mean? Sibling and Parental Appraisals of Childhood Leukemia." *Children's Health Care* 17:22–31.

Davies, B. 1987. "Family Responses to the Death of a Child: The Meaning of Memories." *Journal of Palliative Care* 3:9–15.

Davies, B. 1988a. "The Family Environment in Bereaved Families and Its Relationship to Surviving Sibling Behavior." *Children's Health Care* 17:22–30.

Davies, B. 1988b. "Shared Life Space and Sibling Bereavement Responses." *Cancer Nursing* 11:339–47.

Davies, B. 1990. "Long-Term Follow-Up of Bereaved Siblings." In *The Dying and Bereaved Teenager*, ed. J. Morgan. Philadelphia: Charles.

Davies, B. 1991. "Long-Term Outcomes of Adolescent Sibling Bereavement." *Journal of Adolescent Research* 6:83–96.

LaTour, K. 1983. *For Those Who Live: Helping Children Cope with the Death of a Brother or Sister.* Dallas: Latour.

McCown, D. 1987. "Factors Related to Bereaved Children's Behavioral Adjustment." In *Recent Advances in Nursing Series: Caring for Sick Children*, ed. C. Barnes, 85–93. Edinburgh: Churchill-Livingstone.

McCown, D., and B. Davies. 1993. "Patterns of Grief in Young Children Following the Death of a Sibling." Paper presented at the meeting of the Association for Death Education and Counselling, Memphis, April.

Martinson, I. M., B. Davies, and S. G. McClowry. 1987. "The Long-Term Effects of Sibling Death on Self-Concept." *Journal of Pediatric Nursing* 2:227–35.

Rosen, H. 1986. *Unspoken Grief: Coping with Childhood Sibling Loss.* Lexington, MA: Heath.

CULTURAL, PHILOSOPHICAL, AND RELIGIOUS PERSPECTIVES ON DEATH AND CHILDREN

Children and Death: Diversity in Universality

DONALD P. IRISH

Children reflect their distinctive cultural and ethnic backgrounds in their understanding of death. Both the United States and Canada have become home to an increasing number of people who treasure and honor their past. (It is estimated that, by the year 2010, 35 percent of the U.S. population will be Hispanic and another 20 percent Chinese, Japanese, Korean, or Vietnamese.) Thus, recently, there has been a resurgence of ethnic identity concerns. To understand and support the children who are seeking their ethnic roots and commemorating their heritage, we must delve into their singular literature, stories, and rituals. Above all, in a pluralistic society, we must "ask questions, listen, and find ways to adjust practices and traditions to accommodate their *value systems and needs."*

Donald P. Irish, Ph.D., professor emeritus of sociology at Hamline University in St. Paul, Minnesota, is an editor of Ethnic Variations in Dying, Death and Grief: Diversity in Universality. *He is coauthor and editor of* Death Education: Preparation for Living. *Irish served as president of the Minnesota Coalition for Death Education and Support.*

There are only two events that each of us must experience: our birth and our death, with "living" in between. A traditional Buddhist legend, "Parable of the Mustard Seed," conveys this universality and inevitability well:

> A young woman, Kisa Gotami, grieved greatly over the recent death of her little son, whose body she carried in her arms. Not accepting death as a terminal event—at least for this lifetime—for his "malady" she sought a cure that would restore him to life. She approached the Buddha, known for his miraculous powers to heal. The Buddha provided her with a solution, but not the one she sought. The Buddha suggested that she visit each home in the village to find a few grains of mustard seed. However, she should accept the seeds only from a household in which no one has ever died—not a parent or a child, a servant or an animal. Visiting each home, she found not a single residence in which the death of a member had not been experienced. She learned that death is inescapable for all creatures. Relieved of false hopes and needless grief, she went with peace of mind to the "burning ground" and submitted her son to the cremation fires.[1]

The universal and unavoidable experience of death has produced highly diverse responses both within and among cultures throughout history. In some, the reactions are stoical and fatalistic; in others, extreme emotional expressiveness and deep, long-lasting grief are the norm. The spirits of ancestors are believed to be directly influential in some societies but exist only in the survivors' memories in others. While some cultures foster fear of death as an enemy to be avoided, others may view it, at least in some circumstances, as a friend. A stress on the "here and now" pervades some societies, while others focus on preparing for a "life hereafter." Children are sheltered from death in some societies and are very familiar with it in others.

Two bedtime prayers taught to many American children illustrate contrasting emotional emphases regarding death, apprehension, and assurance:

Now I lay me down to sleep.
I pray the Lord my soul to keep.
If I should die before I wake,
I pray the Lord my soul to take.

Angel of God, my guardian dear,
To whom His love commits me here;
Ever this night be at my side,
To light, to guard, to rule and guide.[2]

Whereas these children's prayers exemplify contrasts *within* a dominant culture, an anecdote that illustrates differences *between* cultures relates to a Chinese servant "who wanted time off to go to a funeral of his cousin. His grudging employer asked him how soon he thought his [relative] would eat the bowl of rice he planned to leave at the graveside. His answer: About the same time that your aunt who died last week smells the flowers you placed on her grave."[3] It is difficult for those of one culture to appreciate the rationale for the behavior of others.

Teaching Children about Death

In the past, most American children were not "protected" from the realities of death, and confrontation with it became an integral part of their informal education. This is still true for some children today: those in urban ghettos, in some rural areas, on American Indian reservations, and within Hispanic communities of the Southwest. The affluent young, on the other hand, are often protected even though vehicle accidents, drug overdoses, and suicides affect them as well. Most deaths are made as invisible and nondisrupting as possible, sequestered in sterile hospital rooms, taking place mostly among strangers in unfamiliar surroundings.

For children without firsthand knowledge of death and bereavement as well as for those with it, children's books can be a valuable tool. Adults must, however, be aware of the biases that these books can transmit. For example, most books about death for young readers, explicitly or implicitly, pertain to "model" children who have two parents (and often a grandparent), reside in a nice home, are white and middle class, and live in comfort. Sexist, religious, ethnic, and racial biases can be present as well.

When children's book expert Sheila Schwartz was a high school student, she recalls that "there were no Jews in children's books, no Blacks above the menial level, no real Indians but only the fantasies of James Fenimore Cooper. Parents in these books were usually affluent, understanding, and urbane, and the girls were all blue-eyed, golden-haired."[4] Nevertheless, stories from African-American, Jewish, Native American, or other ethnic groups within America or other countries can be found, and they can usefully convey attitudes toward death, describe funeral rites, indicate culturally appropriate emotional responses, and explain philosophical or religious ideas that are distinctive to their culture.

For example, in *To Hell with Dying*, Alice Walker records memories of her relationship with old "Mr. Sweet," a guitar-playing man on a neglected cotton farm down the road from her family. Illustrating black Southern patterns of caregiving, she and her siblings rejuvenate the dying old man with their affection over and over again as his death approaches.[5]

In *Season of Discovery*, by Gloria Goldreich, Lisa has her bat mitzvah and celebrates Hanukkah. As a young volunteer she reads to a Holocaust survivor, who dies of a brain tumor. The story indicates how youngsters may usefully relate to those who are elderly, ill, or dying.[6] Another good story in the Jewish tradition is *Bubba, Me, and Memories*, by Barbara Pomerantz, in which her grandmother's death affects a young Jewish girl's life. The narrative highlights family traditions and attitudes as family members sit shivah (observe the seven-day condolence period), recite the kaddish, and reenact other mourning customs. They focus on memories, the free expression of sorrow, and an acceptance of death as a part of life.[7]

A widely read Native American story, *Annie and the Old One* by Miska Miles, involves a Navajo (Diné) girl, her mother, and her grandmother. While Annie's mother is weaving a beautiful rug, the grandmother urges Annie to observe the process. One day the grandmother calls the family together and informs them that she will be "returning to Mother Earth" when the rug is completed and taken from the loom. Alarmed, Annie proceeds to unravel the rug to prevent her grandmother's death. The grandparent discovers the actions and explains that all things come from the earth and return to it. Annie seems to comprehend and develops an awe for life and death.[8]

While respectful, sympathetic, and engaging, *Annie* illustrates the problems that can arise when authors lack sufficient expertise with cultures not their own. It contains numerous inaccuracies regarding Navajo culture. Teachers and parents should be cautious about materials prepared by people who write about cultures that are not their own.

Children and Death

Beverly Slapin and Doris Seale point out that the story gives little feeling of tribal life. The language is halting and stiff. No summer house or shelter is provided the weaver. The "traditional" dress, hairstyles, blanket designs, pot decorations, and moccasin patterns are not Navajo. A Navajo grandmother would not sit with her legs crossed. The bone structure in the faces is not Navajo. There is no fire pit in the house floor. Only the elders wear traditional clothes every day. A Navajo child in the traditional setting would react to death not by acting out but by "shutting down," closing up. [9]

In Eve Bunting's *The Happy Funeral*, a contemporary Chinese American girl and her family observe the death of the grandfather with a combination of traditional Chinese and Christian religious practices. She is told that, "when someone is very old and has lived a good life, he is happy to go." The events experienced together celebrate her grandfather's long life rather than his death. She helps in preparing the funeral and rituals at the cemetery. [10]

In *First Snow* by Helen Coutant, the grandmother of a Vietnamese Buddhist family in New England dies. Lien, age six, asks her mother for permission to light an incense candle to honor her grandma. Her parents indicate that dying means that "things are not really gone; they only change," for Buddhist belief is that "life and death are but two parts of the same thing." Lien understands that death can be seen as a natural part of life. [11]

Reincarnation is more specifically illustrated in *The Mountains of Tibet* by Mordicai Gerstein. In the story, a little boy enjoys flying his kite, but he longs to live in other lands and with other peoples. When he dies as an old man, he is offered choices for his future after death. He decides to be born again. Given the chance to be a boy or a girl, he chooses the latter. Later, there is a little girl born in the mountains, and she loves to fly kites. [12]

Nonfiction books can be useful to children as well. Herbert Zim and Sonia Bleeker's excellent book *Life and Death* describes the body disposal customs among the Iroquois, Maori, Hindus of India, African Pygmies, Navajo, and Chuckchee. Mourning patterns around the world and the variety of beliefs about death are included. The material is scientifically oriented and deals with the physical and biological facts of life and death for plants, animals, and human beings.[13]

Books on dominant white Christian culture are also available, and they too should be read for a full picture of American life. However, since those resources are readily available and identifiable, I will not consider them here.

Children's Roles in Some Contemporary Cultures

Like philosophies of death, the roles that children play in death and funeral customs differ among cultures. Few resources that describe these differences are available, but I will summarize several of them here.

Mexico. Latin Americanist Barbara Younoszai published the following account of rural Mexican funeral customs in 1993:

> Children are socialized early to accept death in a very informal way. They are trained and expected to be part of the wake and of the church service. They also go with their parents to the burial site for yet another ceremony. When the body is lowered into the grave, relatives often take a handful of earth and throw it on top of the casket. . . . *Novenas* are said during the nine-day period following the death. . . .
>
> In rural areas, where the body is viewed inside the family home . . . people chat and talk. Not much ado is made over the body itself. . . . People may occasionally go and look at the deceased, but for the most part they are talking and socializing, with the children running about.[14]

The Day of the Dead in Mexico (31 October–1 November) is dedicated to a celebration of death. There are many kinds of confections and other things for children in the form of skeletons, coffins, masks, and skulls. There are paper designs of Death doing everything and anything that people do. Families position orange flowers on the doorstep in remembrance of a deceased child and also place similar floral decorations on the little graves. A special food is prepared for the day— the child's favorite—and the *pan de los muertos*, a holiday bread that varies by area. Emotions are openly expressed.[15]

Hmong in Southeast Asia. Bruce Thoupaou Bliatout describes traditional Hmong customs, which are shaped by the culture's belief in reincarnation:

Children and Death

As the time of death grows nearer, family members gather around the sickbed. They give comfort and tend to the needs of the dying family member and gain mutual support from each other. . . . Family members and members of the community make great efforts to visit a person prior to the person's death. One of the important reasons for this is the belief that part of a dying elder's skills, abilities, and goodness will be imparted to those who are there at the time of death. Another reason family members come is that dying elders who are able to talk often pass on parts of the family oral tradition at this time.

Children are directly and usefully involved in the funeral process. They serve as firewood gatherers, water carriers, and rice pounders for the community gathering:

Funerals are part of normal village life and children participate in all aspects of funeral activities to the extent that their age and abilities allow. . . . Hmong society . . . puts more emphasis on male youths learning how to conduct and perform the many funeral ceremonies and rituals. Each extended family encourages younger generation males with the aptitude to study some aspect of the funeral rites. . . . Girls and women learn how to behave and help in funeral activities through watching and helping their mothers and aunts. . . . Through constant exposure from childhood to adulthood, the Hmong funeral customs become ingrained in Hmong youth.[16]

Native American–Lakota. Martin Brokenleg and David Middleton describe the way Lakota children in the northern U.S. plains states are educated about the community's grief practices:

Members of the community learn through observation of rituals and verbal instruction by elders. Because people attend wakes and funerals from early childhood onward, they observe how they are expected to behave. . . . By virtue of attention, one will know all one needs to know. . . . This formal but indirect style reaffirms the values and beliefs of the community so that all may be mindful of life's purposes and the necessity of grief.

Mourning is considered natural, and the unrestrained expression of grief is appropriate and regarded as a good thing for both sexes. . . .

There are certain taboos that surround social occasions. To conduct oneself in any way less than virtuously is unacceptable at any time . . . because the family depends on each of its members to personify and perpetuate the proper Lakota life-style. . . . This is especially important for the development of the youth.[17]

Muslims in Iran. As Farah Gilanshah writes, among the Muslims in Iran, children are taught that life has purpose, is brief, and ends in death. Within Muslim culture, death and dying are discussed quite easily, by pupils in schools and within families. Children reared in the West do not talk about dying and death as often or with as much understanding.

Muslim leaders teach that people will see their children and their wealth at the last moments of life:

> Parents will tell their children, "I loved you all very dearly and I was very protective of you. What do you have for me?" The children will answer, "Nothing"—and they cover the grave. Then the person sees all of his or her wealth and goods from this world, and says to the wealth, "I always liked you and sought you out, and I was never satisfied. What do you have for me?" The response will be "Nothing." Then the person will look at all of his or her actions and tell the actions, "I never paid attention to what I have done, and I always misused you in any way I wanted, wrong or right. What do you have for me?" And the actions will respond, "I will be with you on the grave, in the afterworld, and on the day of judgment." In other words, what we take with us from this world are our actions.

At the time of burial, all the family members and friends gather with a religious person. They pray and ask God for forgiveness. No discussion goes on, just crying and praying, because it is believed that people should weep and release their sorrow.[18]

Children, Violence, and War

In every society, adults try to protect children from direct contact with violence. This does not mean, however, that children should not learn about the violence and suffering that other children experience. This is particularly important now that television programs, movies, video

Children and Death

games, and other media provide abundant, unrealistic exposure to violence for most American children. No discussion of children and death in diverse societies can be complete without an account of the violence and war that affects so much of the world.

A number of fiction, nonfiction, and autobiographical accounts accessible to children can teach them about war. Regarding the Holocaust, the well-known account of Anne Frank in Holland has received worldwide acclaim. She manifested the capacity of the human spirit to survive even when confronted with evil.[19] In *The Last Butterfly* by Michael Jacot, a clown of Jewish extraction is forced to entertain Jewish children in Terezin before they leave for Auschwitz.[20] A nonfiction book, *I Never Saw Another Butterfly*, contains poems and reflections by some of the fifteen thousand children who passed through the Terezin concentration camp, only one hundred of whom survived. One excerpt, written by fifteen-year-old Petr Fischl before he perished, reads as follows:

> We stood in a long queue with a plate in our hand, into which they ladled a little warmed-up water with a salty or coffee flavor. Or else they gave us a few potatoes. We got used to sleeping without a bed, to saluting every uniform, not to walk on the sidewalk and then again to walk on the sidewalks. We got used to undeserved slaps, blows, and executions. We got accustomed to seeing people die in their own excrement, to seeing piled-up coffins full of corpses, to seeing the sick amidst dirt and filth and to seeing helpless doctors. . . . From time to time one thousand unhappy souls would come here . . . and another thousand unhappy souls would go away.[21]

The atomic bombing of Hiroshima on 6 August 1945 has also produced a body of literature by and about children. Perhaps the best known is the true story of Sadako and her thousand paper cranes, as described in books by Eleanor Coerr and others.[22] Sadako, two years old at the time of the bombing, was hospitalized with leukemia a few years later. A friend encouraged her to fold one thousand golden paper cranes so that the gods would grant her wish to become well again, but she was able to complete only 644 before her death at age twelve. Her classmates contributed the remaining 356 paper cranes for her burial;

later, a monument financed by children's contributions was erected in Hiroshima Peace Park.

In *Unforgettable Fire*, the Japan Broadcasting Corporation collected drawings and statements from bomb survivors. Yasuko Yamagata, in school at the time, reported, "There were few people to be seen in the scorched field. I saw for the first time a pile of burned bodies in a water tank by the entrance to the broadcasting station. Then I was suddenly frightened by a terrible sight. . . . There was a charred body of a woman standing frozen in a running posture with one leg lifted and her baby tightly clutched in her arms."[23]

The more recent Bosnian war is the subject of *Zlata's Diary*, written by thirteen-year-old Zlata Filipovic.[24] In an appearance before the U.S. Congress, she granted that at "any moment we could be killed." She vividly delineated the war's injustices. "Normal people always suffer." "I have the strength that my parents put in me. It's probably some kind of love, because everywhere were evil and bad things. . . . It's not just my story. It's the story of all the children there."[25] "The only thing I want to say to everyone is PEACE!"[26]

In "Strength," a poem in her book *Peace Tales*, Margaret MacDonald illustrates the overarching violence of contemporary human society. She presents a story of animals who decide to see which is the strongest. Each in turn—chimpanzee, deer, leopard, bushbuck, and elephant—demonstrates its specific powers. Then MAN enters the scene with a gun and kills the elephant. The rest of the animals flee, leaving MAN alone. The poem concludes, "He is the one who cannot tell the difference between strength and death."[27]

Suggestions for Parents, Teachers, and Health Professionals

In addition to the information that parents, teachers, and other professional practitioners can distill from the foregoing materials, I offer the following suggestions for relating to children of cultures other than one's own:

1. Children coming from different cultural backgrounds have had divergent experiences related to death. Age level is not necessarily an

accurate predictor of sophistication regarding exposure to dying and death.

2. In working with people of another linguistic group, communication problems are sometimes more difficult than the cultural differences, although the reverse may more often be the case. Bilingual interpreters from the other culture can help avoid misunderstandings and hurt, especially for the highly significant meanings of death.

3. Avoid conclusions based on minimal knowledge about another culture's beliefs about death. Instead, ask questions, listen, and find ways to adjust practices and situations to accommodate an individual's value system and needs. It is important to understand the answers to such questions as, What are the significant features of a culture's view of death? What are its philosophy and religious views, its customs? What has been an individual's informal "death education"? What rituals and emotional expressions are appropriate in a given culture? One needs the responses not only of adults but also of children.

4. There is considerable diversity *within* common ethnic categories. Thus, guard against broad generalizations. For example, Hispanics may be Cuban, Mexican, Puerto Rican, or from some other Latin American culture, with different customs. The ways of life among the peoples of Southeast Asia are even more diverse. A given child, however, may not represent the "modal" portion of his or her cultural spectrum, and partial assimilation into the dominant culture may have already begun.

5. Although grief is a normal reaction to the death of a loved one, people belonging to cultural minorities, especially recent immigrants to a country, may be grieving for significant losses on a chronic basis— loss of former homeland, family members, personal possessions, economic status, professional identity, language, traditions, and sense of self. These collective losses will also affect the children.

6. To bring children to an understanding and acceptance of dying, death, and grief, be honest regarding your own knowledge, ignorance, and uncertainties. "I don't know" can often be the best answer to some questions. "*I* believe *this*, but *they* [of a different culture] believe *differently*" is an appropriate and culturally sensitive response that does not denigrate the genuinely held beliefs of others. Share books and films

that convey a range of beliefs, depict the rituals, and reveal the emotional expressions surrounding death and dying; these can vivify for children a broader spectrum of perceptions and stimulate their own thinking regarding the variety of patterns possible.

Conclusion

In his classic children's story *Charlotte's Web*, E. B. White handles death sensitively.[28] Although the pig, rat, and spider have different lifestyles and cycles, love and tolerance enable the three to be friends. After Charlotte's death, the pig and rat can share their grief and their memories of her. They know that life goes on, that intense grief is temporary, and that each new generation represents a legacy for the future of us all. Children need to understand these profound insights incrementally as they increasingly take charge of their own lives. Sooner or later we all "go down," white, yellow, red, black, or brown, as Peter Meinke expresses in this poem:

The Mouse You Found

Yes, the mouse you found
is broken, snapped out of breath
by the copper rib; and yes,
we all break sooner or
sooner in the trap of death,
leaving our bones and skin
as crumbling tokens
to be redistributed
by an old technique
to a darker world
where mice don't squeak.

It's too bad. I maybe
write these words
to make me last longer
or, to give me the benefit
of a doubt, to make *you*
last longer; but it won't work.

IT WON'T WORK. You'll find out
that all the mice go down,
white, grey or brown. It's hard,
but it's a quirk
of God.

On the other hand,
we do, after all, live forever
till we die
and after that
who wants to live forever?
Not you, my brown-eyed daughter:
Not I.[29]

Notes

The author expresses his appreciation for the aid provided in the bibliographic search and the advice given by Judy Genk, children's book specialist, the Hungry Mind Bookstore, St. Paul; Julie Rochat and Scott Hanson, reference librarians, Hamline University Bush Library, St. Paul; and especially to LaVonne H. Mayer, Curriculum Lab director, Department of Education, Hamline University, and Lois Ringquist, Children's Department, Minneapolis Public Library.

1. Paraphrased from J. Bruce Long, "The Death That Ends Death in Hinduism and Buddhism," in *Death: The Final Stage of Growth*, ed. Elisabeth Kübler-Ross (New York: Simon & Schuster, 1975), 67–68.
2. Contributed by a "Catholic-Quaker" friend, Pat McGuire.
3. H. S. Schiff, *The Bereaved Parent* (New York: Crown, 1977), 9.
4. Sheila Schwartz, *Teaching Adolescent Literature* (Rochelle Park, NJ: Hayden, 1979), 1.
5. Alice Walker, *To Hell with Dying*, illus. Catherine Deeter (New York: Harcourt Brace Jovanovich, 1988).
6. Gloria Goldreich, *Season of Discovery* (Nashville: Thomas Nelson, 1976).
7. Barbara Pomerantz, *Bubba, Me, and Memories* (New York: Union of Hebrew Congregations, 1993).
8. Miska Miles [pseud.], *Annie and the Old One* (Boston: Little Brown, 1971).

9. Beverly Slapin and Doris Seale, *Through Indian Eyes: The Native Experience in Books for Children*, 3d ed. (Philadelphia: New Society, 1992), 191–92.

10. Eve Bunting, *The Happy Funeral*, illus. Vo-Dinh Mai (New York: Harper & Row, 1983).

11. Helen Coutant, *First Snow* (New York: Knopf, 1974).

12. Mordicai Gerstein, *The Mountains of Tibet* (New York: Harper & Row, 1987).

13. Herbert S. Zim and Sonia Bleeker, *Life and Death* (New York: Morrow, 1970).

14. Barbara Younoszai, "Mexican American Perspectives Related to Death," in *Ethnic Variations in Dying, Death, and Grief*, ed. Donald P. Irish, Kathleen F. Lundquist, and Vivian Jenkins Nelsen (Washington, D.C.: Taylor & Francis, 1993), 76–77.

15. Barbara Younoszai, "Hispanic Perspectives Related to Death" (1991, typescript), 17–18.

16. Bruce Thoupaou Bliatout, "Hmong Death Customs: Traditional and Acculturated," in *Ethnic Variations in Dying, Death, and Grief*, 85, 95.

17. Martin Brokenleg and David Middleton, "Native Americans: Adapting Yet Retaining," in ibid., 105–6.

18. Farah Gilanshah, "Islamic Customs Regarding Death," in ibid., 140; see also pp. 142–44.

19. Anne Frank, *The Diary of Anne Frank: The Critical Edition*, comp. Netherlands State Institute for War Documentation, trans. Arnold J. Pomeras (New York: Doubleday, 1989).

20. Michael Jacot, *The Last Butterfly* (New York: Bobbs-Merrill, 1974).

21. Hana Volavkova, ed., *I Never Saw Another Butterfly: Children's Drawings and Poems from Terezin Concentration Camp, 1942–44* (New York: Schocken, 1978), 14.

22. Eleanor Coerr, *Sadako and the Thousand Paper Cranes* (New York: Putnam, 1977). See also Toshi Maruki, *Hiroshima No Pika* (New York: Lothrop, Lee & Shepard, 1982).

23. Japan Broadcasting Corp., ed., *Unforgettable Fire: Pictures Drawn by Atomic Bomb Survivors* (Tokyo, 1977), 52–53.

24. Zlata Filipovic, *Zlata's Diary: A Child's Life in Sarajevo* (New York: Viking Penguin, 1994).

25. "Her Eyes Have Seen the Horror," *Minneapolis Star Tribune*, 11 March 1994.

26. "A Child's Diary of War," *Newsweek*, 28 February 1994, 27.

27. Margaret Read MacDonald, *Peace Tales* (Hamden, CT: Shoe String, 1992), 12–17.

28. E. B. White, *Charlotte's Web* (New York: Harper & Row, 1952).

29. Peter Meinke's "The Mouse You Found" is reprinted from his *Trying to Surprise God* by permission of the University of Pittsburgh Press. Copyright © 1981 by Peter Meinke.

Behind Smiles and Laughter: African-American Children's Issues about Bereavement

WILLIAM LEE JR.

Many African-American children in the inner city are exposed to constant violence and death. Their smiles and laughter become a mask for explosive anger and unresolved grief. For good reason, the national Centers for Disease Control have declared violence a public health epidemic. The true victims are children. The moving narratives presented in this chapter challenge us to understand and to assume responsibility for children who grow up in an environment of turbulence and crisis.

William Lee Jr., Ed.D., is the president of Implosion, Inc., the Center for the Studies of Death, Loss and Bereavement. A licensed teacher, death educator, mental health counselor, and marriage therapist, Lee presents programs internationally that are related to death, loss, and violence. He is co-chair of the Crime Task Force of the city of Cambridge, Mass., a member of that community's Crisis Response Team, and commissioner of the Mayor's Commission on Unity and Justice. His varied activities put him at the forefront of the community when crises arise.

Many African-American children in the inner city are exposed to constant violence and death. Their smiles and laughter become a mask for explosive anger and unresolved grief. For good reason, the national Centers for Disease Control have declared violence a public health epidemic. Its true victims are children. The moving narratives presented in this chapter challenge us to understand and to assume responsibility for children who grow up in an environment of turbulence and crisis.

In America our children represent all cultures and all socioeconomic, family, religious, and geographic groups. Children's reactions to events are influenced by values, perceptions, information processing, and membership functions within their groups. It is important and worthwhile to examine children's responses to death and loss and how they make meaning out of and cope with life's stressful events. However, not all analyses apply to all children; therefore, we must approach these explorations through diversity's pathways. This chapter will focus on inner-city African-American children's responses to death and how we can help them manage their losses.

A Viewpoint on Children

Years ago, as a substitute teacher fresh from college, I overheard a third grader's comment to a mother who was a lunch monitor: "Mr. Lee . . . oh, he's a friend of children." I was quite pleased to hear that comment; in fact, it helped me choose to begin my professional work with children facing death and loss. Once I realized that services to assist children in coping with death were limited, I tried to expand their scope. Since that time, many children have provided me with unique opportunities to share in their thoughts and feelings about death and violence.

Many years have come and gone since I began working with children. Since I left the classroom setting, the roles have been reversed, and children have become my teachers. My current teachers are the African-American children of the inner city.

Children of the Inner City

Many complex issues are associated with understanding inner-city African-American children's responses to death, loss, and violence.

Usually, inner-city children are assessed in terms of their behaviors alone, without consideration of the context in which those behaviors occur. But such assessments must incorporate anthropological and sociohistorical perspectives, or they will present a fragmented, incomplete view. These children's reactions do not occur in a void and mean more than the behaviors themselves suggest. My intention here is, therefore, to take a closer look at the construction of reality that produces these behaviors. The diaspora of a people is the beginning.

The African Diaspora

The term *diaspora* refers to the dispersion of a people, whether forced or by choice. Usually, the people so affected share similar roots and experiences and are therefore very likely to react to events in similar ways. However, economic, social class, religious, and geographic differences can also color people's perceptions and therefore shape an individual's reactions. Once we get past the commonalities of the African-American experience, we see that the responses of inner-city children to pain and grief cannot be understood from a monocultural perspective alone.

Keeping this caveat in mind, one of the most important effects of the diaspora is the forced slavery of African-Americans in the Americas. The African-American response to slavery was to deny feelings, a learned response that was necessary to survival under slavery. Such behavior has been historically transmitted, resulting in a construction of reality that remains today a central motif of African Americans' core experiences, particularly experiences of death and loss.

Socioenvironmental Context

The African-American child in the inner city is bombarded daily by violence and death, real-life experiences that are reinforced by continual media presentations of violence and death. Early in life, the inner-city African-American child develops ways to resist the daily mental and emotional intrusion of provocative material. Sometimes the coping strategies utilized are not healthy, often because the choices are limited. Take, for example, hypervigilance. A child may choose hypervigilance because it gives him or her the feeling of control and safety. I have a friend who lives in a high-crime neighborhood, where gunshots and shootings are common occurrences. She reports that her three-year-old has reacted in a specific way ever since gunshots were unintentionally fired into her living room. Every time my friend's daughter hears a loud noise, she is already poised for action, and, if the sound resembles gunshots in any way, like a car backfiring, she hits the floor, her body flat out.

I wonder about this child's potential for trusting or for developing images of the world as a safe place. At three years old, freely exploring one's environment is developmentally appropriate, yet this child is hyperalert and believes herself to be in harm's way. What types of relationships will she develop? What messages will she transmit to her peers and children? How can she develop empathy and compassion if trust is eroded at such an early age? The first building blocks of self-esteem are put in place as we come to value ourselves, who we are, and how things ought to be. Fostering those feelings used to be a major function of the family, extended families, and the community. In the postmodern, high-technology world, however, family and community have changed. In many instances, the inner-city parent is struggling to survive, making choices as basic as those between fuel to keep a child warm and food to keep her or him from hunger. Meanwhile, for a large percentage of inner-city African-American children, socialization takes place during unsupervised television time, and the culture to which they are exposed there is one of death and violence.

Inner-city parents rarely have the chance to take recreational trips that would expose their children to positive experiences and counteract the negative experiences of inner-city life. Opportunities to view different approaches and choose the ones most acceptable are also limited. In the inner cities, ways of thinking are usually singular, and alternatives aren't available. For example, one view of "respect" prevails if someone "disses" you; if in return you do not beat him down, you are considered a punk, not a man. That viewpoint is strictly enforced, and alternative ways of thinking are unacceptable. Once established, the norms become rituals that are fixed and rigid. These norms are reinforced by peers as codes of honor and conduct, "the way we do things in the 'hood." They are modeled and then copied by wannabes and younger children, and the cycle is established and perpetuated in the stories and behaviors of urban warriors and street gangs. How we feel about ourselves profoundly affects how we connect with and disconnect from significant people, including how we learn to manage loss.

Inner-city children are in particular need of understanding. Their voices are not often heard. While I cannot delineate all the issues involved, I can outline the sociohistorical context that continues to underlie their social construction of reality. An understanding of this construction is essential to informed treatment.

Who Are These Children?
The Inner-City Imploded Child

Who are these children in our inner cities who have observed firsthand physical assault and other violent losses? On first glance we might expect to see children with saddened, depressed, and perhaps tearful expressions. However, smiles and laughter often mask confusion, self-fragmentation, structural disorganization, and pain—underlying rage so disorganized and explosive that, once released, it can no longer be controlled.

Many of these children appear to be uncaring, cold, and distant when faced with loss. They smile and laugh when talking with friends about violence and violent death. Unfortunately, because they so successfully cover their true feelings, these children are likely to elicit negative reactions when they encounter individuals involved in the helping professions—and certainly not the empathy and compassion that they need most. When they meet with such rejection, the consequences are long term and severe. These are the children who are having children—throwaway children who, without intervention, create another generation of the same.

Why do these children react the way they do? Their method of handling loss helps them stay in control. To acknowledge loss is to come into contact with their underlying rage, and that prospect fills them with anxiety. Furthermore, the peer culture in the inner city does not respect outward displays of empathy and compassion, which can connect others with feelings that they cannot control, and children are therefore fearful of exposing themselves and their feelings.

Human resource and helping professionals are often afraid to deal with others' anger because it releases and unlocks their own unresolved rage. The very thought of losing control, an American obsession, is met with immediate distancing and denial. So, in the inner-city community, when an African-American child gives even the slightest signal or hint of anger, he or she is met with the message that it is inappropriate to express that anger; and children who cannot suppress their anger are likely to be identified as problems.

Usually, children who have been physically and sexually assaulted, or exposed to violent death, have little or no opportunity to express feelings of anger, violation, or abandonment safely. Over a period of time they become victims of the fear of internal upheaval. They become anxious to keep the lid on this uncontrollable emotion.

These children need opportunities to communicate with others who have had similar experiences. When that occurs, they can observe within others a part of themselves. They can then understand what a normal reaction to an abnormal situation is. Healing can begin with the sharing of experiences, speaking about the unspeakable, empowering the self to name those events, making meaning of the meaningless. The affirmation of each other and the normalization of these children's feelings through schools, agencies, and helpers' empathy and compassion provide safe places with boundaries. And, once anger is properly elicited, helpers can coach children in the verbal or artistic rather than the physical expression or denial of feelings of loss.

These historical and sociological factors play an important role in the formulation of behavioral responses to death and loss. I now share some case histories as well as some of the children's actual responses to questions about death. All the children discussed are from the inner city. Names and other personal identifying characteristics have been changed to protect the individuals.

James

I met James when he was in preschool. He was five and a half years old, and his father had just died. James's behavior was described as disruptive and aggressive. He always had to be first in line, and he became extremely upset about losing anything, even a simple game. He would hit and fight other children at the slightest provocation. His paternal aunt with whom he lived reported episodes of uncontrollable rage when he was required to do anything that he did not like. He displayed active suicidal gestures in the form of verbal statements and trips to the rooftop of the housing project where he lived. He also had nightly conversations with his "dead" father. These conversations were comforting and provided relief from continuing thoughts about his father's death.

His teacher reported that James was unable to concentrate on minor tasks that required being still for a few minutes. When he became upset in class (a frequent occurrence), he would lose control, displaying a strength driven by the energy of rage, and he could be restrained only with the assistance of an adult male. The principal and James's teachers suggested that his father's death produced behavior that placed him at risk of committing acts of violence to himself and others, of being labeled as having attention deficit disorder, of using drugs as a way to numb his feelings of anxiety, of dropping out of school early, and of using and abusing sex to compensate for other feelings.

James's story recalls two other case histories.

Michael

I met Michael when I was a substitute teacher in the Boston school system. Being new, I was assigned a class with children who were described as difficult and incapable of learning. My job was to keep them quiet and busy; teaching was secondary. After half an hour I decided to have all the children come together into a group and talk.

While the class was scampering to form a circle, I noticed a young boy who appeared to be dozing. I had a child next to him touch the sleeping youngster and asked him whether he was ill or just sleepy. The child responded that he was daydreaming. "What were you dreaming?" I asked. He said he did not know. I asked him if he had always daydreamed. He answered, "No." Since when had he, then?

"When my brother died. And I been daydreaming ever since."
"How old was your brother?"
"Three years old."

"How did your brother die?"

"Some kind of a cold." (Pneumonia, I thought.)

"How old were you at the time?" I asked. He said he did not remember. I asked him what grade he was in. "First grade," he said.

"Six years old?" He nodded.

I was very angry. Here was a young boy labeled as uneducable because no one had even asked what was troubling him.

One year later, when I began to focus on death as a topic, my experience with Michael came vividly to mind. Had educators been familiar with death and children, had they understood that this young boy might have been at a developmental transition point and used distancing through daydreaming as a coping method, they might have perceived that Michael probably felt responsible for his brother's death. Perhaps he had directed angry thoughts or intentions at his brother. Children often believe that their thoughts can cause certain events to happen. The guilt associated with being responsible did not give this child the opportunity to relieve himself of his painful mental state. In addition, he may have been made to feel even more guilty by comments from adults, such as, "If you had placed the blanket on your brother when I told you to, maybe he wouldn't have caught cold."

If Michael had received special bereavement counseling, it could have alleviated some of his guilt and aided parents and family to better understand him and help him adjust as he survived the experience of losing someone close. Thus, the developmental growth of this young boy would have been nurtured rather than retarded.

A few years later I encountered a similar situation.

Anna

Mrs. Jones was an inmate at a women's prison. She had been in counseling therapy with me for nine months before I met her children. She had three daughters, the youngest of whom was nine-year-old Anna.

Anna spent a great deal of time with Mrs. Jones's mother and father. Since her mother's incarceration when Anna was seven, Anna had adjusted well. She was described as a polite and considerate youngster. When I met her six months prior to the incident reported here, I found this description of her to be accurate.

Approximately four months later, Mrs. Jones's father died. Two months after his death, Mrs. Jones's mother wrote her daughter concerning Anna's behavior, which she described as quite different than usual.

For the past four days, Mrs. Jones's mother reported, Anna had been unmanageable. A letter from Anna's school revealed that her grades had dropped in five subjects. She was put back in math class, and she was glad of it. The main issue was "much sass, no respect, anything said to her, her answer is 'So what.'"

Her grandmother reported that she had spoken with Anna for three-quarters of an hour: "I asked her to tell me what was troubling her. Her very words were, 'My grandpa is dead; my mother is in jail and may die before she can come home. What will I do?'"

What about more recent cases? The following cases were observed in 1992 at an inner-city school in a high-crime neighborhood. These are African-American preteens who have recently experienced the deaths of parents or siblings. When the reported behaviors were observed at school, several faculty members did not agree that they were related to death events in students' lives. For many of us, it is often easier to categorize problem behaviors as "the way they are" than to probe more deeply for a cause.

The following excerpts all describe behaviors most frequently observed among these African-American middle school students.

Ramos

Ramos was fourteen years old when I first interviewed him. He was a small, slender young man for his age. He was very anxious and continued to play and focus on an object that he moved from hand to hand. Both parents were HIV positive intravenous drug users. His mother had been hospitalized recently. Ramos was explosive and often lost control of himself. He abused classmates and constantly destabilized the environment. His communication skills were poor, and he used the classroom to socialize or act out. The observed behaviors increased with his mother's hospitalization and impending death.

Alice

Alice was a thirteen-year-old black female whose brother had recently been killed. While interviewing her I discovered that Alice had experienced the deaths of six persons she had some relationship with: two boyfriends, two cousins, one brother, and a grandfather. I found Alice to be a pleasant, cooperative, and caring young woman. However, these attitudes were not displayed in her daily interactions at school. She was described at school as a loud student who took everything personally, an attention seeker who often came to class late. She had constant conflicts with others, usually involving fighting. This constant strife with peers and resistance to authority demonstrated a great deal of anger. Her behavior affected the environment negatively.

In our conversations, she was easy to engage and talked freely about the many losses in her life. She shared many reflections about her behavior: about "not being able to sit still when all of a sudden thoughts about her brother would come into consciousness" or that "in the neighborhood girls want to be tough, therefore you must be tough." I have interviewed and worked with many young people. I sincerely believe that this young girl did not want to behave in physically aggressive ways to resolve disputes, but she felt that she had to.

Alice taught me another lesson when she showed me that there are creative and private ways that children cope with loss. Alice shared with me her photo album, which she kept in her school locker and carried with her from class to class. In the front of the album were pictures of school friends, family members, birthday parties, and holidays. Toward the back were five obituaries. She said that she kept the obituaries there so that she could review them as needed and remember the love she had for the people she had lost.

Jane

Jane was twelve years old when I interviewed her. She was alert and well dressed, attentive and relaxed. Her grandfather's death was difficult, she said, because he "really loved me." Jane was described as lacking confidence, not attending to instruction, often daydreaming, constantly seeking one-on-one attention, and frequently socializing in class. She was perceived, however, as a likable student.

Ralph

Ralph was a fifteen-year-old student. During the interview he joked and was purposely silly. He did not want to discuss his brother's death and resisted any gentle probing. He immediately began to distance himself by changing the topic. Ralph was described as very quiet, withdrawn, and very well mannered. He appeared troubled, however, his facial expressions indicating that he was distancing himself from his present environment.

These are some examples of typical behaviors observed in five children as they reacted to the deaths of significant people in their lives. I now present comments from children on how they would respond to the deaths of parents and significant others. These children are from the inner city and all attend city public schools. They are representative of the same environments, schools, and economic circumstances as the children discussed earlier. The excerpts will be identified by the child's grade, gender, and age. These children were asked to respond to the question, "If one of your parents died, how would you feel? What would you do?"

Grade 6, Female, Age Twelve

"I would be mad, scared that someone would try to split up my sisters and brothers and me. Scared, confused, lonely, sad, angry. Scared what might come if my father died next. Confused about whether to believe it or not. Lonely about that one of my parents are gone. I would get a chance to talk to them no more. Sad—about—that they died, and angry that they had to die. I would try to face up to it. Try to realize that it happens. Go on from where I started from and try to live.

"People could be there if I need someone to talk to. People cannot tell the social worker because that would be in your business, checking out the other parent, and if that parent isn't doing well, they would try to take the children away from their parent. Relatives cannot fight about what was left behind—they should not be happy.

"Teachers should not yell at you and not push you so hard. When you are not doing your work as fast, they would not yell at you because you are slow and would be easier on you because you are trying to concentrate—it is hard to concentrate on one thing when you are thinking about another, and the tercher should try to understand what you are going through.

"I will be more angrier, I would yell more, be more crankier, and be rude, if someone tries to be nice, I might snap at them. I would not be able to concentrate on anything because I would be thinking about two things, the schoolwork and them dying. Would fight. . . . If someone said something about them, the first reaction is to jump up and punch them in the face."

Grade 6, Female, Age Twelve

"Sad, lonely because they died, they are parents, I would cry, I wouldn't go to school because I would not be able to concentrate, because I would be thinking about my parents. I would be thinking they died, I would not want to concentrate—I would not care about things, just wishing my mother and father would come back to be with me again because I loved them.

"Other people can do nothing, just leave me alone, because I would be mixed up thinking about what would happen to me. I wouldn't know who I would live with or what would happen to me. I want relatives to help me to get over it. [How?] Want to live with them, be somebody, provide love, food, clothes, and somewhere to live. Love first, someplace to live second, food third, clothes fourth—because I wouldn't have that."

Grade 6, Male, Age Twelve

"I don't think I could accept that—I would probably have to live with relatives. . . . Usually when I have problems, my mother is always there. . . . I don't think I would accept that. I wouldn't feel good for a long time, I probably would lock myself in my room. [Why?] Because I really would not want to see anyone for a while until I get over it. Then I would have to choose who to live with. I would be angry and pray to God and say 'Why?'—my mother and I are very close—I would be angry at God for letting my mother die. Would be angry at everybody for a while. I would be really mad at God and mad about death . . . because if they didn't have death then she would not have to die. I'd probably be sick for a while. [How?] Like a mad sickness.

"It would be hard for me to accept that I would be angry at people—would yell at them . . . tell them to leave me alone. Other people can start caring for me again. When I have a problem, they can work it out with me and help me with it. Teacher can try not to remind me of my mother, treat me the same and don't mention about my mother. I would try to be good and don't get in trouble so people wouldn't ask for my mother. I would try to work things out for myself."

Grade 6, Female, Age Eleven

"Like crying . . . feel sad and wish she was still alive because I am close to my mother and father . . . would feel hurt because it's my mother . . . wanting to see her because they might be mistaken, it might not be my mother . . . would want to know how she died. Just to know, because if someone asked, I would know.

"I would cry, would want to be with my father instead of being with myself. I would be afraid to be by myself because I would see her in my mind and it would make her feel sad.

"Would want other people to not talk about it around me because I would feel sad. Want someplace to stay, take care of me. [How?] Giving me a place to sleep, something to eat.

"Teachers can try not to talk about the subject of death. [Student began to cry.] I would ask people not to talk about death. When someone talks about my mother dying I would get mad. . . . I would cry and ask the person not to talk about it."

As we have seen, these children's responses are very similar to the behavior of children who had actually experienced the death of significant people. The following case gives an even more detailed picture.

A Mother's Observation of Her Four-and-a-Half-Year-Old Son's Reaction to the Death of His Father

Author: . . . If you could just generally talk about what's been happening and questions and other kinds of stuff and what you think about it and what the reactions were . . . and that will be fine.

Mother: Well . . . it was times when he would just start talking about his father, and he would ask if he was in heaven, and I would tell him, "Yes, he went to heaven," and he would go outside, and he would get things from. . . . He would tell the kids, "My father went up," and they would say, "Your father didn't go up, he went down," and he'd get very disturbed and run in the house. There was a book that I showed him that angels and stuff going up, and he would come in the house and get the book and take it back out there an' show it to the kids, and they would say, "You know, that's just nothing, you know."

A: What was his first reaction when you informed him about his father?

M: His first reaction was, umm, well, the way I explained it to him, I couldn't say, "Your daddy's dead." I didn't tell him that his father was dead. I told him that his father went to heaven. And he looked at me, he was like, you know, he didn't say anything. I said, "Your father is gone to heaven." He says, "What?" I said, "Your father's dead," point blank. I came out with it like that 'cause he didn't seem to understand what I was saying when I told him his father went to heaven.

A: And what was his response to that?

M: His response was, "What happened to my daddy? Who took him to heaven?" and I told him, I says, "Everybody has to die one day, you know they die, and if they good, they go up, if they['re] bad, they don't go up," and he asked me what happened to him, and I told him that his father died from drinking. You know, he was drinking, and he just laid down, and he went to sleep. He asked me if he would ever see him again, and I told him no. So he wanted to uh—a day after that he didn't say too much about it no more that day. The next day, he came in the kitchen where I was, and he was kinda [whining?], and he said that he missed his father, and I told him that you can't see your dad, he's dead, and I said there's no way you're gonna be able to see him no more right now. So he ran in the room, and he got a photo album that we have pictures and stuff. He wanted to get the picture of his father, and he went through the photo album, and there was one picture in particular that he likes where his father sent him that you know [with] muscles and all that kids get [flattered?], and he couldn't find it, but he did find some other pictures, and he just looked at his father's pictures, and he just started crying, and he came in the bathroom and just kept crying. He kept saying, "I wanna see my dad," and I said, "I told you," and I kinda got aggravated with him at that point. I say, "I told you that your father was dead and you're not gonna be able to see him no more, so let it go." You know, 'cause he was like going on and on and on with it like. And it was disturbing me because I didn't know what to do. I felt bad for him and everything, and that was his first reactions. You know, he didn't understand that his father wouldn't be back to see him anymore.

A couple of days after he had died it was time to be going to pre-school, 'cause I think that happened on a Saturday, and T. was going to be going to school that Monday, so that was the Monday morning when he woke up, and he wanted to see the picture photo albums and kept crying and everything.

He wanted to go and get his clothes that his daddy had bought him. You know, he said, "My daddy bought me this." He wanted his hockey shirt, you know, he was—my daddy—he didn't want nothin' that I had bought for him 'cause and his father became a big issue. He kept saying that he loved him, and he asked me if I loved his daddy, and I told him yes I did love his daddy. He said well why couldn't— you wouldn't let him stay here? And I explained to him. I said, "Your father had an alcohol problem, and we couldn't live together, but I did still love your father, and we, you know. . . ." He says, "So my daddy wasn't a bad man, he just was bad when he drank, right?" I said yes. You know, those were some of the questions that he would ask me, and, umm, he asked me, why did God kill his father, and I told him no, God didn't kill his father, I said, you know, I tried to explain to him that this is Satan's world and everything and that God didn't kill him, and I said, "You be a good boy, maybe one day you'll see your father again," you know.

"Everybody has their turn, you know, to die." But he was under the impression that if we died that we would be with his father, you know. Questions like that kinda bug me because I don't want him to think that we was going to right away try to die so we could be with his daddy.

A: Can you kinda talk a little bit about some of his reactions? Can you talk about some of the events that followed? So you would think there is some depression? What does he do when he gets silent?

M: He just sit there, and he looks like in another world for a few minutes, he do.

A: Have there been issues about his own death that he has raised? Have there been nightmares, have there been? . . .

M: No, he don't have nightmares. He sleeps well; he just made accusations from time to time.

A: What are those accusations?

M: That we—he wanted me and him to die and go be with his father, he wanted to be with his father, you know? If we die we wanna go be with his daddy. He say, "Momma, I hope we die so I can be with my daddy," and I tell him, I say, "Don't say that, honey, in due time, when God is ready, or when it's time for us to go, we'll go, but we not goin' try to rush it." I say, "Your father didn't try to rush his life, it just happened."

A: Maybe in those times and events, one might say that there is no real guarantee that if you die that you will see your father or rejoin him, I can't promise you that.

M: Well, I try to make it easy for him cause it look like he doesn't want to hear any negative.

A: Well, you see, but what he is trying to say is, he is of the belief that if he dies he will reconnect with his father. And what one needs to say, the way I think is, one needs to say to him that there is no guarantee.

M: Keep on saying that you're gonna see him one day, you know, because that's what he expects.

A: Right, give him hope, but also I think it's important with the issues of if I die, I can join my father, I think it's important to break into that and say, you know, that there is no guarantee.

M: Right, hmm.

A: Well, this is normal, when the child loses one parent, the child has a fear that the loss of the other one is imminent, so the child may become more clinging and more, you know—

M: Yeah. He's afraid of losing me, he doesn't want me out of his sight, you know, because of what happened to his father.

A: It's a natural thing. Talk somewhat about some reactions at the dinner table. I remember you told me some comments and stuff that he had made right after the funeral?

M: Oh yeah. He said his father's hands were cold. He asked me, I didn't even know that he had touched his father's hand at the funeral, you know. He asked me why was his daddy's hands cold, and I told him that they have to put you in freeze, they have to freeze you to preserve you while you're out. And he said, "But they was hard," and I said, "Well, that's the way it happens." I said, "He doesn't have any life in him now, so when they freeze you, your hands get cold and hard," and stuff like that.

A: How did he accept that? What was his impression of the graveyard and funeral?

M: I feel that I was protecting his hurt. He was hurt, and I wanted to comfort him, and that was the only way I could see comforting him without—the fact that he knew that his father wasn't going down in the ground. It seemed like it was disturbing him to know that his father was. . . . He would say, "My daddy go down in the ground, he's going to be with the devil, but if he go in the sky, he's going to be with God." So it made him feel relieved that his father was going to heaven.

A: But it appears from your facial expression that you're kind of tormented a little with how much am I lying and deceiving my child and how can I protect my child from the hurt and am I really a bad person?

M: I was trying to protect his feelings. I didn't think I was bad; I was protecting him. Hey, I had—I can't stand to see him like that too, you know. It was hard enough.

A: But I see some conflict there in you. That's all I'm saying.

M: Yeah. It's a lot of conflict there.

A: I believe you're doing the right thing, and I think that you're struggling like any mother would struggle with her child.

M: But I don't wanna keep telling him that, you know. It was like a fairy tale story. But I figure when he gets older, he'll be more apt to understand more than he would at a point in his life right now. So what I'm trying to do right now is comfort him the best way I know how, and that was. . . . He was making accusations like his father was going down in the ground with the devil, so that made him feel real bad, so I told him he wasn't going down in the ground with the devil, that he was going to go up.

It was always a hope that things would just get normal again and that we could probably make another go of it, but it just seemed like there wasn't enough time. His son . . . and I look at him all the time and I . . . he keep reminding me all the time of him, you know.

A: When you have attachments and love which attach you and bond you to a person, there is a lot that has been between you and. . . . You were connected, and that connection was broken by death when there was always hope of a reconciliation, but with death, there is no hope.

Conclusion

When I began thinking about and writing this chapter, my goal was to engage the reader in a dialogue about inner-city African-American children's views on death. I have presented only my perceptions of their views, but actual voices of children help us answer or at the very least consider the question, "From whose perspective?"

When we work with all children, we must understand that the human face relates to the sociohistorical context. Caregivers must connect with children, by being, if not by doing. We must appreciate each individual voice as well as the pattern arising from these voices that can help us determine central issues relative to death and loss.

Caregivers must be alert to emotional and behavioral indicators that may indicate a struggle with bereavement, such as hypervigilance, distancing and denial, daydreaming, acting out, low self-esteem, and even active suicidal ideation. In seeking to help, teachers must also keep in mind that the factors outlined above, coupled with the unique living conditions in the inner cities, the historical relationship established between blacks and whites, the violence that permeates society, and the patterns of expressions and the ways in which cultural messages are transmitted through nonverbal observed behaviors, may make communication more of a challenge.

Finally, the case studies suggest the following for educational practices and policies:

- The death of a significant other places children at risk within educational settings.

- The educational readiness of children is a direct consequence of how they cope with life's losses.

- Significant loss affects all children at their core, regardless of how they may appear and act. Their words and actions alone are not an adequate basis for assessments.

- Consciousness raising among school personnel about children's reactions to death and loss is a primary task of bereavement professionals within schools.

Bibliography

Achenbach, T. 1982. *Developmental Psychology.* New York: Wiley.
Ammerman, R. T., and M. Herson, eds. 1990. *Treatment of Family Violence: A Sourcebook.* New York: Wiley.

Bowlby, J. 1969. *Attachment and Loss*. Vol. 1 of *Attachment*. New York: Basic.

Erikson, E. 1950. *Childhood and Society*. New York: Norton.

Garbarino, J., N. Dubrow, K. Kostelny, and C. Pardo. 1992. *Children in Danger: Coping with the Consequences of Community Violence*. San Francisco: Jossey-Bass.

Kohut, H. 1978. "Selected Problems of Self Psychological Theory." In *Reflections on Self Psychology*, ed. J. Lichtenberg and S. Kaplan. Hillsdale, NJ: Analytic.

Lee, W. 1987. "Children's Conception of Death: A Study on Age and Gender as Factors in Concept Development." Ed.D. diss., Harvard University.

Lee, W. 1991–93. "Emotional Graffiti: An Expressive Workshop on Anger Management for Children and Adolescents." Conducted at the 4-H Camp, North Carolina Extension Program, North Carolina A & T State University, August.

Lee, W. 1992. "Without Empathy and Compassion: At Risk and Protective, Factors of Violence among Black and Latino Adolescents." Invited paper presented at the Second International Conference on Children and Death at the University of Edinburgh, Scotland.

Lee, W. 1994a. "Issues of Loss and Transition within the Emerging Multicultural and Multiethnic Diaspora." Invited paper presented at the National Conference on Loss and Transition, Boston.

Lee, W. 1994b. "Preparing the School Community to Cope with Violence." In *What Will We Do? Preparing the School Community to Cope with Crisis*, ed. R. G. Stevenson. Amityville, NY: Baywood.

Stith-Prothrow, D., and A. Weissman. 1991. *Deadly Consequences*. New York: HarperCollins.

Protestant Perspectives on Grief and Children

RICHARD B. GILBERT

More than any other event, the death of a loved one raises for people of all ages the most profound questions about good and evil, reward and punishment, and concepts of an afterlife. Although Protestantism encompasses a wide variety of thought and teaching, we present here some general insights on basic theological beliefs and ritual considerations. These perspectives on grief play a significant role in helping the child confront the inevitable moments of darkness and despair.

Richard B. Gilbert, M.Div., is director of pastoral services at the Porter Memorial Hospital, Valparaiso, Indiana. A clinically trained and certified chaplain, a fellow in the College of Chaplains, and a Lutheran pastor, he has long been active as a grief educator, counselor, author, and advocate. A bereaved parent, he has traveled widely to give presentations and talks on spirituality, pastoral care, and grief, has published many articles, reviews, and chapters, writes columns for Bereavement *magazine, is a friend to support groups and individuals in their grief journey, and is a member of the boards of the National Catholic Ministry to the Bereaved and the College of Chaplains. He is finishing his first book on the spiritual connections in the grief journey.*

How can I explain Protestant perspectives on grief, especially as they apply to children? *Protestant* has at least as many definitions as the hundreds of denominations under its umbrella. To suggest even such a definition as, "Christian, but not Roman Catholic," would not satisfy some members of the Protestant family. To avoid getting sidetracked in dogma or church history or disputing parts of the content presented on the basis of individual preferences, belief systems, or customs, let us, at least for the sake of the children in our care, set aside the contentiousness long associated with Protestantism (we do "protest"). Let us use the resources that are part of our characteristic pathways and varied traditions to discuss the needs of the bereaved, most especially, our children.

Relationship

Protestants range from having a guarded distance in their relationship with God to having a highly personalized, indeed, intimate, relationship with a "personal Savior." While its intensity may vary, the fact of relationship is common to Protestants. Our understanding of God is one of salvation, of a loving, caring, remarkably active, and intimate God who so loved us that "he gave his Son to die for us." That is the theology, and, translated into promise, it is, as Saint Paul would remind us, the truth (and hope) that "nothing, not even death, will ever separate us from the love of God in Christ Jesus our Lord" (Rom. 8:38–39).

Experientially, it is this concept of relationship that children understand. Even when the adults in the lives of children overlook the children's ability to perceive and express matters related to grief, relationship is crucial to understanding Protestant bereavement patterns. We are in relationship with God because God has called us and claimed us. That is the relationship. Death comes. A human relationship is interrupted by death. We grieve. We are ultimately carried through to healing, which is remembering, because death never interrupts the relationship God has given us.

What is this relationship about? Like other Protestants, I have many memories of my days in Sunday School (a trademark of Protestantism I examine later). One memory stands out as both significant to the discussion here and crucial in my own journey of faith and life.

On the stage in the Fellowship Hall (all Protestant churches seem to have one of those) of my home congregation is an enormous picture of Jesus. It is known as *Jesus, the Good Shepherd.* As an adult, having measured the picture and realizing it was twelve feet tall and on a very high stage, I could understand why it looked so big. To a very small youngster, it was enormous. Yet it was never frightening, only comforting. The picture first became important to me when, as a third grader, I learned of my adoption as an infant. It was an issue that would haunt me for a long time. Still, even in the pain of sorting out the ramifications of adoption, it was Jesus, the Good Shepherd, who always was the source of my strength, my boundaries, my relationship. It became meaningful for me as well as part of my motivation for ministry. To a little boy, however, it was all about relationship. It was Jesus carrying the lamb and Jesus carrying me. I was in that picture, and I still am. It wasn't an idle wish, or even a threat on my part, but hope, built on a promise, that later I would understand as God's grace (grace is an important word for Protestants) claiming me, adopting me, as his child. It is that relationship that sustains me, keeps me going, through all the mountains and valleys of life, even those shrouded by death. We may come to our understanding of relationship in many different ways. Most mainline Protestants see that relationship as God's gift to us, based on his love, offered in the baptism of infants and children. Others stress "believer's baptism." But the common thread through it all, and something that children certainly understand, is relationship.

A death is the interruption of a human relationship—whether through a sudden death in an emergency room; a lingering on through disease, perhaps in a nursing home or hospice; or the stealing away of the breath of life in pregnancy. Painful interruptions, wrong, by human standards, are a part of life, the created order. We grieve, we hurt, we lash out at the God we want to blame for all this. We feel abandoned by the one who has died, by the people who offer meaningless or hurtful comments, by the people who stay away or even feel abandoned by God. The relationship tells us that God never abandons us. It is the crucial factor of salvation as a gift, as Protestants understand it, that makes the difference when we grieve.

When we affirm these dynamics of relationship with adults, we can also begin to realize that the concept of relationship is also a human expression, and we are reminded of bonding, or basic trust, which begins at birth. It is about the nurturing of parent to child, sibling to sibling, friend to friend, neighbor to neighbor. Children understand what it feels like to belong, what it feels like to have a relationship interrupted (we break up those fights over shovels in the sandbox and basketballs in the gym), but children also have learned, by experience, by observation, and, as they grow, by faith, the meaning of relationships that continue despite the human experience, even the experience of death.

Children may not understand the concepts of eternity, forever, death (when we think about it, most adults still struggle with those concepts), but they know what it means to belong. In this age of abusive and disrupted relationships and communities, we know what it feels like to feel abandoned. Adults want to belong. Jesus is the gift that assures that. Children want to belong. Jesus is the gift that assures that they do.

Resources

Protestants have great symbols of their faith and practice that become gifts to God's children of all ages. Again, Protestant groups vary in their interpretations of symbols. So I will describe a middle or general course that readers can adapt to their personal beliefs.

Baptism. Through the sacrament of Holy Baptism we are claimed and assured of an eternal (i.e., permanent or constant) relationship with a loving God. Death does not interrupt that. Rather, it is one stage or transition in that relationship. When we talk about death, we remember our baptism and that we belong to God.

This important tenet of faith is crucial, for it is about relationship that goes beyond death. It is about trust in that relationship despite what may come during the course of life. This does not mean that everything that happens to a person is the "will of God." We must avoid explaining or justifying tragedy in this way. When my wife and I became bereaved parents, it was of no comfort at all when others told us, "God knew best," or, "A loving God had some wonderful purpose in all of this for us." If I had not used the resources of my faith in other ways, explanations like these could easily have caused me to walk away from a God who could not possibly be a "loving God" and still take away my child. This death was not right or just. Loss is loss, not a matter of right or wrong. I worked recently with a family whose boy was killed in an automobile accident when his car skidded on a patch of ice on the highway. Another auto fatality. His tragedy did lead to viable organ donations, but does that justify the death in the sight of the parents or of God? Of course not!

The "will of God" is not a hiding place. We hide (i.e., seek refuge) in the embrace of the God who understands even when we don't! It is one thing to hide in that embrace. When we try to hide in some religious rhetoric that justifies this death, it offends both what the deceased means to us and the meaning of God in our lives.

Most of all, while the whole discussion of the "will of God" can be purposeful at various times in our grief journey (sometimes the only thing we have is the privilege of asking the unanswerable "why?" questions), it is not an answer at all. The healing in grief comes, not because of answers, but because of remembering despite everything that is unanswerable, unjustified, inescapable, and beyond explanation.

So it is important to offer the resources of faith not as definition or explanation but as reassurance and nurturing to sustain us in our sorrow. It is important that we help bereaved children understand the promises of relationship (which children can understand), even when it is impossible to understand the reason some things happen the way they do.

We are beginning to heal when we move beyond blame or explanations to claim memories and stories. We want to avoid the two extremes of "God wanted your loved one with him in heaven" (regardless of the pain it causes you) and "God has nothing to offer to you in the crisis of your grief." There is a hymn that so beautifully expresses the sentiment of faith in the midst of grief, faith as trust rather than explanation:

> Children of the heavenly Father
> Safely in his bosom gather,
> Nestling bird nor star in heaven
> Such a refuge e'er was given.

> Neither life nor death shall ever
> From the Lord his children sever;
> Unto them his grace he showeth,
> And their sorrows all he knoweth.
> (Caroline V. Sandell Berg, trans. Ernst William Olson)

The Bible. Again, Protestants differ among themselves in their understandings of the Bible. For some, "it is the divinely inspired Word of God," correct down to "every jot and tittle." Others use tradition and reason along with scripture to sort out word and meaning for today's world. However one views the scriptures, they are surely a means of communication, of maintaining relationship, of guiding us, directing us, strengthening us, and, yes, even correcting us, so that we can live in the relationship that God has given us.

Children treasure their books. My daughter Allison is twenty-three, and busy working on her graduate degree. Her room may still be "off limits," but I know that somewhere in there are the very first books we read to her as a child. Television, boom boxes, and home videos may have displaced much of our reading, but we are surrounded by words and messages and are ever aware of the power of communication, even when we do not communicate well. Sometimes we can communicate across the globe more effectively than we can with the most important people in our lives, but we know what *word* means.

The Bible serves as a word—for some, "*the* Word." But for all of us, even children, it is a word that is a resource for understanding, comfort, and strength. We do not know why some things happen as they do (we just have to read through the Psalms to discover that we stand in a long line of people with similar experiences and the same questions), but we can open the Bible and read, "In my house are many mansions," and know that, even if seemingly pointless, there is some direction in that loss. We can wonder if anyone understands the pain we are feeling, and our Bible will tell us, "Jesus wept," or, "Blessed are those who mourn, for they shall be comforted," and thereby experience a God who has "been there" then and is "with us" now. Our baptismal rite reminds parents about reading to their children. It says it differently ("Put into their hands the Holy Scriptures"), but children understand words, communication, sharing, telling, listening, and being open to messages that comfort and carry.

Religious education. Protestant churches take great pride in their educational programs. They boast of "classes for all ages" and provide for religious education in various forms. They have a wonderful opportunity to teach and nurture children in matters related to loss and grief. Whether it happens is another matter. Because we respect teaching and the inclusion of children (and their needs and issues) in that framework of education, we should take seriously that children need to be included in the grief process and share in our mourning.

We often fail to maximize our "teachable moments" when it comes to grief and instead reinforce the erroneous notion that grief is an adult issue. Still, Sunday School teachers do have the opportunity not just to teach children facts but to nurture a relationship that is sustained, despite our losses and crises. For many adults raised in the Protestant tradition, the concept of Sunday school is inextricably bound up with memories of loving, concerned teachers they knew as children rather than specific theological tenets. My favorite Sunday School teacher is now eighty-five years old. When I go back to Messiah Lutheran Church, she may be proud of me as the pastor and chaplain, but what makes it all so important between us is not my master's degree in theology or my ordination papers but the love of Jesus we knew (and still know) as teacher and child.

Hymns. Protestants like to sing. As an organist, I am thrilled when I have a good pipe organ and a congregation ready to sing the great hymns of the church. For many Protestants, their devotional life is as steeped in the tradition of hymns as it is in scripture. I have worked in many nursing homes with people afflicted with many expressions of dementia. They seem to respond to nothing in the way of human inter-action but sit up and react when a familiar hymn or carol is sung. This is the incredible power of music, the power of words, the power of faith.

Many hymns relate to children as well as to matters of faith and grief. All products of a Sunday school education learn "Jesus Loves Me, This I Know," and it is sung with "knowing" expressed less in terms of intellect and more in terms of experience of covenant or community. We "know" because we "experience." Songs are sung in Sunday School and worship, at retreats and campfires, and at home; many families have some kind of hymnal or Christian songbook on the piano or elsewhere in their home. Preachers regularly quote hymns, the great poetry of the church, and share the stories that accompany so many of them. The hymns are powerful because so many emerge from the human struggles with life and faith. They offer the assurance of Christ from people who have paved the way for us through the pathways of life.

Henry Lyte gave us most powerfully a statement of faith, set to music, about the "eventide" of life. While too many hymnals seem to place it in the section termed "nighttime," this hymn is about eternity, moving beyond the "last night" to the eternal light. He writes,

> Abide with me. Fast falls the eventide.
> The darkness deepens, Lord, with me abide.
> When other helpers fail and comforts flee,
> Help of the helpless, oh, abide with me.

Children understand dependability, keeping one's promises, the fear of darkness, of being disappointed when people have failed to help. The words may be for adults, but young children often understand better than adults what Lyte, writing about strength of faith experienced in a dying friend, is saying:

> I fear no foe, with thee at hand to bless.
> Ills have no weight, and tears no bitterness.
> Where is death's sting? Where, grave, the Victory?
> I triumph still if thou abide with Me!

The Lord's Supper. Holy Communion is central in the worship experience for many denominations, as an expression of the "real presence" of the living Christ. Rooted in the Passover story relived in the Upper Room the night before Jesus died, the communion meal is the gathering of God's people around the table of the Lord. That is something all Protestants should understand. The mechanics and depth of meaning vary among denominations, but all God's children understand gathering around the table to eat. Even in this fast-food, poor nutrition age of ours, we know what it is like to feel hungry and to be offered bread. Jesus identifies himself as "the Bread of Life." He tells us that those who believe in him will never be hungry or thirsty. Bread and water sound simple when we are used to pizza, hamburgers, and soft drinks. Some eat; others don't. These are matters of taste or preference. All our standards are cast aside when we look to Christ as the spiritual bread for us.

When we grieve, we are hungry, hungry for understanding and being understood, for comfort, for someone who will listen and, perhaps foolishly or as a desperate plea for hope, someone who will make sense out of all this. In a familiar New Testament story, two men walked on the road to Emmaus. They were trying to make sense out of what they had just experienced. Jesus offered neither words nor explanations. In fact, he waited ("he wasn't known to them") until they stopped explaining and were willing to enter into relationship and experience. They gathered for something as basic as an evening meal after a tiring day. It was there, in the meal, that they realized that they were with Jesus. Revelation. Relationship. Again, we are back to the basics of Protestantism and bereavement experiences. We know what it is like to hunger and to thirst. So do children. We need to include them when we gather around the table, whether it be "the Lord's Table," as some refer to the altar, or the family dining-room table when neighbors are bringing over those endless tuna noodle casseroles that Darcie Sims mentions (see the bibliography). They are part of the family, including the family of believers. Maybe if we would remember to include the children, we would also understand that they have much to teach us.

Prayer. When the disciples said, "Lord, teach us to pray," Jesus offered them the "Our Father." It was a model for our prayer life, that which is intended to keep us focused on God as Parent and to help us realize the experiences of faith throughout life and throughout life's needs and struggles.

The key to prayer is not in the script but in the focus. When we teach children about prayer, we need to be teaching them that prayer is primarily a matter of keeping doors open with God. We all know Dennis the Menace, cartoon rascal. Perhaps he was right in one portrayal of him with his nighttime prayers: "It is good to have friends in high places." Yet prayer is not manipulation but a way of maintaining relationship, a "no holds barred" conversation, believer with God, God with believer.

Every letter I receive from a bereaved parent says somewhere, "Chaplain, how do I pray again after my child died? Does it mean anything to ask God to watch over my other children after this happened?" How would you answer them? Is it a prayer problem or a faith/trust problem? Of course, each letter I receive is a little different. What is essential is that children often know the simple truths of prayer better than adults. We cloud prayers with religious jargon and other clutter. Children are straightforward. "God, I am talking to you. I have your undivided attention. This is what I have to say. What do you have to say to me?"

Responsibilities

As Protestants, we are responsible for using the various resources available to us to deepen our own faith experiences and especially those of our children. Death and its subsequent grief ministry is taken very seriously by God and needs to be taken equally seriously by the church.

Many clergy and other religious leaders, members of various congregations, and clusters of churches and religious individuals are doing splendid work in grief ministry. Many congregations provide space for and encouragement to support groups; many church-related publishing houses are printing excellent materials and resources for the bereaved. There are Christian social workers who teach about grief and songwriters who are composing helpful music. There are many, many individuals who through their willingness to walk with others, or to share their stories, provide ministry to the bereaved. So many of the best and most popular books on grief are not academic ones but the ones of people simply sharing their story because it is a gift to their healing and from their healing journey to others.

Overall, however, Protestant grief ministry is, at best, short-sighted and narrowly focused. Most people gather for the visitation and service, maybe even providing a meal in the church after the funeral, and help out briefly in the weeks that follow. Then little else is done, and people often feel forgotten by the very people (and the God they represent) who ought to do better.

As Protestants, all the resources cited earlier are also mandates: Bible, prayer, sacraments, hymns. They all talk about grief taking time and about how the church needs to provide support and care.

Protestants have great opportunities to provide grief ministry. Other books are available on the subject, including those cited in the bibliography at the close of this chapter. The question we must answer is, "What are we doing for the bereaved?" not, "How well do you do funerals?" Does your church library have books on grief, books that are appropriate given the loss experience and the age of the reader? Over the course of a year I preach or teach in dozens of congregations, and have seen probably fifteen grief books as a sum of their efforts. Do you hear sermons that affirm that grief is normal, that feelings of anger are appropriate—even anger toward God? Are you told that the pain of grief is part of the love that is in that story, that God affirms grief, and that the Christian community ought to be setting the trend in providing a loving and nonjudgmental arena for the bereaved? I hear those sermons at funerals and occasionally on Easter or All Saints'. Until through preaching, teaching, and interactions with people the church says, does, and shows, "The bereaved are welcome here," the people will turn elsewhere for information and support and possibly never address the crucial dimensions of grief. The majority of the inactive members in our congregations are so because of some reason related to loss. It really says something to us about how we ought to be conducting ministry and evangelism.

The church has wonderful opportunities and very clear mandates to pursue bereavement ministry. It is for the elderly woman whose husband of fifty-three years has died; it is for the parents whose baby dies of SIDS; it is for the little girl whose brother has died and wonders if she is still a sister. It is for parents dealing with empty nests, for the young person dying of AIDS, for children dealing with broken marriages or absent parents, for people without jobs, for those who suffer from various diseases. Grief is there. What may not be there is the opportunity to mourn. It is necessary for all people, including God's people, and for people of all ages.

Risks

When the religious community moves into any kind of ministry, including ministry to the bereaved, it comes with all the baggage of our own stories as well as the traditions of our own denomination or faith group. We may be religious communities, but, like all communities, we suffer the influences of society and societal pressures, culture, language, and ethnic backgrounds. Lutherans understand this, which is why it is often hard to get us to agree on many things. A joke told in one congregation may bring uproars of laughter and do absolutely nothing in another congregation of the same denomination, simply because, culturally, the people in the second congregation do not give themselves permission to laugh in church.

Geography plays a part. Denominations within our country are different within themselves, differences based on location as well as ethnic and cultural background. What are comfortable subjects to address either individually or within the congregation in one group are not acceptable in other circles. What are customary reactions to the bereaved in some communities are totally different in others. These are part of the risks and challenges that we must respect if we are going to move the church into bereavement caregiving.

There are other risks. Some churches offer commitment to children in name only. Children are still silenced, much like women often are, and, until those churches are restructured (freed up), children will seldom be given an opportunity to grieve in a healthy way within their community of faith. If there is a clear division between adult issues and children's issues, the children will lose.

Some communities can be abusive and addictive in their control of people and what they believe. The bibliography suggests some helpful readings on this subject. You must ask whether your church allows you to freely question God, to ask where God fits into your crisis or loss, to express that you are angry with God and that the crisis of your life does not seem to fit with your understanding of faith and the promises of God. (You might want to read some of the writings by Leo Booth on the addictive and abusive use of religion.) Those questions show not a lack of faith but rather the courage and freedom of faith that allows you to bring yourself, and your pain, before a loving God. Many churches crush that spirit, often smothering it with very dangerous comments about the will of God. Saint Paul suggests that God's will, that is, purpose, is to reveal the secret of the mystery that God loves us and has assured us of that love through Jesus. Nowhere does Paul, or anyone else, say that this means that God is no longer a mystery.

God is God. We are his children. We do not always know the will or whereabouts of God. This ignorance is revealed in the "why" questions we ask. "Why did God let our baby die?" When we scoot off to grab our Bibles to "find" an answer, we not only distort the Bible and God's will but also show that we do not understand grief. There are no answers to those questions, but people ask them to tell us that they hurt, that they want to find meaning and faith in their grieving, and that they want people, and God, to listen. If people are not free to raise the experience of grief as part of faith (not contrary to it), then there is a problem in that religious community that needs serious attention.

Earl Grollman tells the story of a visit he made to a group of ministers to talk about grief and their grief experiences. One minister, making very clear that he knew Jesus and felt very comfortable with the Bible, said, "I don't understand why we have all of this talk about grief. We are Easter people who know an eternal life. Therefore, we should be happy when someone dies. *Besides, no one ever comes to me from my church to talk about grief.*" Are we surprised?

Here is another example of poor grief ministry, of closing the door that God and the bereaved are trying to keep open. It was a tragic death that brought some people to our emergency room one Christmas, death by violence. All of us raged at the suffering of someone so young and so innocent. It was unfair, and we wanted, even as health care providers, to find meaning and comfort in that impossible moment of pain.

As the chaplain, I stepped aside to allow the family's minister to do grief work. It was the proper protocol but a tragic mistake nonetheless. The minister didn't assess the situation and certainly did not grasp the reality of *ministry as presence*. He forced his agenda immediately on the family. He addressed his need to do something, never checking out with the family what they wanted or needed. For example, for them a prayer at that moment might have been offensive or unwelcome. He was doing rather than being with and destroyed a golden moment for ministry to the bereaved. Over the shouts and sobs, he shouted even louder, and with very evident annoyance, "Let us pray," and continued (without even waiting for "permission"),

> Gracious God, we know you hear us over these very loud and intrusive noises. We are sorry that this boy died, but are glad that you chose this time to "take" him from us. We are so pleased that you tell us we live beyond death, and that Christians have hope, not sorrow. The little town was noisy that first Christmas. It is very noisy here. May we all be silent and hear the singing of the angels. Amen.

He then smiled at the people, shook their hands, and left the room. The readers will have to decide how frequently these events occur.

All too often, ministers "drive by," offer some official rhetoric, verse or ritual, and then leave. What this minister failed to do was to understand that, for that family, prayer was already taking place in the very wailing to which he objected and that he could have enhanced or blessed had he simply appreciated the reality of God's presence. The minister's presence was a silent, but very visible, reminder of the presence of God. The minister had tremendous resources available, including the one he used. The disappointment was that he was determined to be directive, instead of walking with the people in their sorrow. Every tear, every sigh, every word, every expression, they were all prayers, all conversations with their God. Maybe the family needed reassurance and clarification (when they were ready for it), but they did not need an "official" prayer that somehow came from a higher authority. Ministry of presence is about listening, waiting, respecting the silences, and, as the family (or individual) moves with the minister in that journey, to do prayer, to do communion, to do confession, to do ritual—together. God is always willing to wait. Why do we seek to hurry either God or the person en route to God? If God isn't in a hurry, and if the greatest gift we can give to the bereaved is time, then why do we need to rush into prayer, sacraments, or other actions? It is again our need to "do" rather than the bereaved's need for us to be with them. It is important for that minister, and for all of us, that we continue to reflect on our agendas, our own grief issues, and the issues or stumbling blocks that place themselves in the way of presence. Some of the best prayers I offer at the bedside of a dying patient and with the patient's family are never "said" by me at all. God is with us when we are willing to struggle with each other, to care, and to be present.

Fortunately, it was a young person, the boy's brother, there in the trauma room, who did the ministry. "Mom and Dad, you taught us both that you will always love us as Jesus does. I am very angry at the guy who did this to Jimmy and don't know where Jesus was in this horrible crime. I just know that Jimmy still loves me, and so does Jesus, and nobody can take that away from me."

Reminders

There are few common denominators when one is trying to explain anything about Protestants, how they believe, or how they behave. For every example cited here there are probably ten exceptions. What is important is that we see the common threads woven throughout the Protestant story, that the very fabric of Protestantism affirms grief, and that children grieve.

The Protestant community has a splendid opportunity, through its understanding of relationship, to speak to and to hear the bereaved of all ages and circumstances. The Protestant community also has, through its strong commitment to education and to preaching, the ability to equip both the bereaved and those who would walk with them to deal with loss and to grapple with faith.

At the heart of the Protestant community is Jesus as revealed to us in the scriptures. He has clearly reminded us that all are important to him, including the children, and that this standard can be no less a priority for his people. Where grief is taken seriously, Jesus is present. That ought to be the watchword for people seeking comfort in their sorrow.

Again, from "Abide with Me,"

Hold thou thy cross before my closing eyes,
Shine through the gloom, and point me to the skies;
Heaven's morning breaks, and earth's vain shadows flee;
In life, in death, O Lord, abide with me.

Bibliography

Bayly, Joseph. n.d. *Where Is God in All of This?* Available on audiocassette from the Compassionate Friends, P.O. Box 3696, Oak Brook, IL 60522-3696.

Clark, Martha. 1987. *Are You Weeping with Me, God?* Nashville: Broadman.

Gilbert, Richard. 1991. "The Use and Abuse of Religion in Grief." Workshop presentation, the World Gathering on Bereavement, Seattle. Available from the author, Porter Memorial, 814 LaPorte Avenue, Valparaiso, IN 46383.

Kaczmarek, Vickie. 1991. *Rays of Light.* Lackawanna, NY: Community Pastoral Care and Grief Center.

Keller, Paul. 1988. *Living the Promises of God: 365 Readings for Recovery from Grief and Loss.* Minneapolis: Augsburg Fortress.

Musser, Linda. 1991. *God Is a Birdwatcher.* Omaha: Centering.

Rupp, Joyce. 1988. *Praying Our Goodbyes.* Notre Dame: Ave Maria.

Sims, Alicia. 1986. *Am I Still a Sister?* Albuquerque: Big A.

Sims, Darcie. 1994. *If I Could Just See Hope?* Albuquerque: Big A.

Chapter Nine

Life, Death, and the Catholic Child

MARY ANN McLAUGHLIN

Any explanation of death requires a frame of reference.
For Catholics, that frame of reference is the life, death, and
resurrection of Jesus Christ as it is realized and celebrated in
the Church. This mystery, expressed in the funeral rites, informs
our faith as it is lived in the most ordinary circumstances.
It offers Catholics a foundation for exploring the reality
of death with a child.

Mary Ann McLaughlin, M.A., is an associate director of the
Office of Spiritual Development in the archdiocese of Boston.
She is a graduate of Boston College's School of Education with
a master's degree in Christian spirituality and a certificate of
spiritual direction and retreat direction from Creighton
University in Omaha, Nebraska. Mary Ann and her
husband, Tom, are the parents of six grown children.

I was twenty-seven years old when my mother died. My oldest son, John, was five. For the fourteen months prior to her death our family had been preoccupied with her care. The children were always around, but I was very distracted. One morning after her death, I found a small photograph of her under my son's pillow. At first I left it there without mentioning it to him. I remember being overwhelmed with a feeling of sadness. It was such a simple, poignant gesture, expressing his grief, that it touched deeply into my own grieving. I could have ignored it, and in a way I wanted to, but eventually I did ask. He told me he was afraid he would not remember her; he was upset that he had not been at the wake or the funeral. He had questions about the funeral, about death, and about God. He wondered, "Where is Nana now?" I thought he had been too young to know the difference. I was wrong! He had found his own way of dealing with his sense of sadness and loss. I must admit that I felt I had missed an opportunity to help him, yet here was an invitation for us both. I responded by using the resources I had, namely, my own faith and belief in God. He still did not understand why he had not gone to the funeral, but, since Nana was with God, it did make perfect sense that he could remember her in his prayers.

I certainly was not prepared to deal with the struggle of a five-year-old trying to come to terms with the death of his grandmother. Yet, in looking back, I am aware of what I wanted to share with him that day, and it was very simple: Nana was happy with God in heaven; God loved Nana very much now as always; and, even though she was separated from us, the bond we had with her in life would not be broken. In retrospect, that conversation put a perspective on my own grieving that helped me remember and pray in the same childlike way. The little photograph stayed under his pillow for a long time, and there were many other questions and conversations that helped his own grieving process as well as mine. One of the things I learned from this experience was that he would continue to probe the mystery of my mother's death as he grew. He would continue to search throughout his life, and the Catholic invitation to life in Christ would continue to aid him in his search.

My husband and I wanted to help our children claim their Catholic identities from the beginning. At the earliest age, we introduced our children to God and to prayer as a way of talking to God. Before they could speak in full sentences, we would show them pictures of God at home or in church and were delighted when they would point and say, "God," in hushed tones. As they got older, "saying their prayers" or "talking to God," in church, before meals, as well as at bedtime, became part of their daily ritual. In very simple ways they would ask God to intervene in their lives, requesting forgiveness, help, and blessings for all aspects of their lives. At the age of seven or eight, the Eucharist became part of their spiritual life, and Jesus' death and resurrection was celebrated with the parish community at Sunday Mass, making Christ's presence and our place in the communion of saints real. The love and care for one another that were celebrated in our family meals and the ordinary day-to-day experiences in the "church of the home" also communicated God's presence. This foundation gave us a frame of reference out of which we could begin to respond to our children in the face of death.

When we are faced with a child's struggle to make sense out of the suffering and death of someone they love, we are forced to draw on longheld beliefs and articulate them in a way that is both consoling and hopeful. That is no easy task. Many of us, as adults, have yet to find the words that adequately express the mystery of death; we find that there are gaps in our own understanding. In addition, when we offer these explanations to children, they can respond with innocent questions that probe the mystery and discourage those of us who are uncomfortable with paradox. We need to understand what we really believe as Catholic adults about life and death as a Christian.

In their book *Christian Life Patterns* (1979), Evelyn and James Whitehead write, "To be appreciated fully at any point in its course, life must be apprehended as a whole. Human life, then, must find its deepest meaning in its relation to death. But death seems to stand as a stubborn impediment to meaning. It destroys plans, it undercuts purpose, it breaks the bonds of love. Humankind has struggled to discern a meaning in life that can prevail against the power of death. In this struggle, Christians have been among the most audacious. For we claim the hope of resurrection. This hope does not void death; death always precedes resurrection. For many of us it does not lessen death's difficulty or lighten its pain. But it rescues death from absurdity."

In dealing with the mystery of death with our children, we deal with the mystery of life and the mystery of God. What we as adults believe and how we live out those beliefs will have a more significant effect on the child's growth and development than any factual explanation we could offer. Therefore, it is vitally important for Catholics to come to terms with what the Church teaches about life, death, suffering, and God as well as how those beliefs are lived out in ordinary life experiences. For Catholics the ordinary experiences of life are intimately connected with God in Jesus Christ. In order to see life and death from a Catholic perspective, it is important to acknowledge the foundation of our belief.

Catholics believe in a loving God who created the universe and breathed his own breath into humanity, making man and woman in his own likeness. The Genesis accounts of creation tell us of a God who is in relationship with man and woman and is present with them in the Garden of Eden. In time, through sin, the relationship is broken; death becomes part of the human reality, and Adam and Eve are separated from God and live in exile. In the centuries that follow, God continues to desire a relationship with humanity and expresses that desire by sending prophets to forge a new covenant. While some people respond, humanity in general is reluctant and always seems to move away from God. Then God sends his only Son, Jesus Christ, born of Mary, a young Jewish woman. In Jesus, the Word of God that was present at the dawn of creation takes on human flesh and enters into the human story. By Jesus' death and resurrection new life is breathed into humanity, giving a meaning to life that prevails against the power of death: "Just as in Adam all die, so in Christ all will come to life again, but each one in proper order" (1 Cor. 15:22). Jesus, the second Adam, lived in ordinary circumstances preaching an extraordinary message of new life: "I come that you might have life and have it in abundance" (John 10:10). His crucifixion and death signify a covenant that promises that, in Jesus Christ, God is with humanity in a new way. Having entered into death, after three days Jesus conquered death in his resur-

Life, Death, and the Catholic Child

rection. After the resurrection, the disciples gathered together with Mary, the mother of Jesus, fearful and unsure of how they would go on with their lives. In this gathering, the Spirit of God descended on them, breathing life into this small community, and the Church, the Body of Christ, was born.

By our baptism we are immersed into the Paschal Mystery of Jesus Christ's death and resurrection and incorporated into the Body of Christ, the Church. The baptismal rite acknowledges that "all who are buried with Christ in the death of baptism rise also with him to newness of life." We are welcomed into the community of faith, that is, the Church, claimed for Christ, and marked with the sign of his cross. As Catholics our relationship with Christ is intimate because of our baptism. We are called to die to sin and rise with Christ daily. We live our lives in Christ through the sacraments, Scripture, and prayer as well as our love and care for one another. Finally, we die in Christ. This dying in Christ makes death different for the believer because Jesus promises us life in abundance with him in heaven.

In the Eucharist, the death and resurrection of Christ is recalled, and by the power of the Holy Spirit this Paschal Mystery is rendered present for the sake of our future. The Eucharistic celebration reminds us of our continuing communion with those who have gone before us. We are part of the communion of saints. This communion with God, in Christ, and with one another is brought to completion primarily in the Eucharist. Both in baptism and in the Eucharist, Christ leads us sacramentally through death into new life.

Our day-to-day experiences also offer us opportunities to practice acts of mortification, small sacrifices that are another kind of dying in Christ that can bring us to new life. As Catholics this is our faith, a graced awareness that informs our life in Christ from beginning to end. This can make all the difference in how we live as well as how we deal with death.

The challenge for all of us is to live out these teachings and explore them in actual life situations. I heard recently of a child who was asking about what happened to his great-grandmother's bones when she was buried. Questions such as these can reflect more than curiosity. They could be the beginnings of spiritual wondering. In this case, four-year-old Jimmy was visiting the home where his great-grandmother had lived, and his aunt was listening to his night prayers. As he prayed for "Gammy," he began talking about her. It was just after Easter, and they had recently visited her grave. He seemed to know that her soul was with God, and this comforted him. In the midst of this conversation came the question, "What happened to her bones?" The fact that his great-grandmother's bones were there, in her grave, did not seem to satisfy him fully. The look on his face and the whispered, "Oh," betrayed that fact. Jimmy finished his prayers and went off to sleep, but the experience left his aunt wondering whether there was more to his question. In looking back, she now sees that his family and the parish school he attended had given him a foundation to explore death from a spiritual perspective, even at such a young age. Having the right answer was less important than her willingness to explore the mystery, share her own beliefs, and listen to how Jimmy saw it all unfolding. Understanding death is a lifelong journey, one that cannot be completed in one day or one conversation. Children raise questions that cause us to reflect and find words to express our beliefs in the face of mystery. How privileged we are to be invited into this part of the journey with a child we love.

One often unappreciated aspect of children's bereavement is the dynamic and concrete character of each child's relationship to God in real-life situations. In *The Spiritual Life of Children* (1990), Robert Coles sees children "as seekers, as young pilgrims well aware that life is a finite journey and as anxious to make sense of it as those of us who are farther along in the time allotted us." The spiritual experiences of the children whom Coles interviewed in his research affirm my own experiences. Coles was at first reticent to pursue a spiritual line of inquiry; he says, at one point, "It's a pity, I now realize, that I didn't explore with that girl in 1965 what ideas she held about God, His nature, His purposes" (p. 65). This reticence is familiar to adults, who realize that delicate mystery in children's conversations yet hesitate to draw it out. Encountering spirituality, or touching that relationship of the human person to God in an actual life situation, can be uncomfortable at times, for it is in our spirituality that we are most unique and at the same time most at one with another person. Children seem to have an innate understanding of this, and the experience of encountering suffering and death early in life seems to tap into this awareness. Coles confirms this, saying, "Children try to understand not only what is happening to them but why; and in doing that, they call upon the religious life they have experienced, the spiritual values they have received, as well as other sources of potential explanation" (p. 100).

Adults must be prepared to meet, not only the physical and psychological needs of children dealing with suffering and death, but their spiritual needs as well. We must listen for evidence of the spiritual life of the child in whatever way is appropriate for that child. Some children are more quiet and reflective, while others work out questions in words, drawings, or play. Children's imagination is engaged as they try to make sense out of painful circumstances. Furthermore, their spiritual questions aren't always articulated in what adults would consider spiritual terms.

The experience of dealing with suffering and death touches the deepest part of our spiritual nature and can bring young and old face to face with the reality of God. How we see God will affect the way we deal with suffering and death. Conversely, the way we deal with suffering and death will affect the way we continue to grow in our relationship to God as well as how our children come to know God.

I was born into a Catholic family and attended Catholic schools. The sacraments, Scripture, prayer, and caring for one another were part of my Catholic identity from my earliest moments. Yet only in retrospect did I realize how these beliefs permeated my family's way of living through death and grief. When I was seven years old, my grandmother suffered a stroke. I remember the strange-sounding malady as coronary thrombosis—big words for a seven-year-old. Since she was paralyzed on her right side and needed constant care, my grandmother came to live with us. Our dining room became her bedroom, with a hospital bed occupying the space where our dining room table had been. Needless to say, our life changed. My grandmother was not one to suffer in silence; she was very demanding, especially where my mother was concerned. I remember her crying in pain and calling for my mother. Every now and then there would be tears in my mother's eyes as she talked about trying to find ways to work it all out. It wasn't easy, but it was a family matter. My aunt and uncle lived upstairs and helped with her care, and even at the age of seven I was recruited to assist with my grandmother. I knew that this time was particularly hard for my mother; she would talk to me about her own prayer and ask me to pray that God would be with us as well.

Our parish priest came regularly with communion for my grandmother. These visits were very special moments for our family, but especially for me as a young child. Great preparations were made. My grandfather's black crucifix was set on a small table between two white candles, and we had special linen towels. The priest would hear her confession privately; then we would kneel and pray as she received the Eucharist. I remember these visits as times of togetherness and great peace in the midst of suffering.

Nine months after she had moved in with us, my grandmother died. We had gone out to buy tires for the car. When we returned, all seemed well, and she was sleeping quietly. The house was quiet, and we were so happy that she was restful that we tiptoed around so as not to wake her. It was much later that night when my mother checked in on her that we realized she had died. I remember thinking how quietly death had come for her.

The priest was called as well as the doctor. When Father McCarthy, our parish priest, arrived, he said the prayers and then sat with us in our living room. Once again there was a pervasive peace in the midst of all that was happening. He talked with us, but most of all he listened. Since Father McCarthy had brought her communion during those months, he was well aware of our family's struggle with suffering and now death. He had journeyed with us, and he would be there at the funeral Mass and in the months following her death, reminding us of the reality of Christ's presence. To a child of seven, he seemed unafraid in the face of death. His presence, as well as his words, assured us that my grandmother was with God in heaven and that God was with us through it all.

My mother talked easily about believing that her mother was at peace, no longer in pain, that she was in heaven, with my grandfather and with God, yet in some mysterious way still united with us. I would later learn that this "connection" was referred to as the communion of saints, experienced most particularly in the celebration of the Eucharist. I remember the sadness and the tears my mother shed; I remember seeing my father with tears in his eyes. Yet their beliefs allowed them to grieve with hope.

The wake was held in the house, so life went on as usual. There were many people—friends, neighbors, and relatives—who came, brought food, made sure we children were taken care of, and kept the vigil with my family. A younger cousin, who was about three, not knowing the finality of death, tried to get my grandmother to wake up and have a cup of tea with him. That story is still told some forty years later. In those days, death had to be contended with in the midst of day-to-day living.

Now I realize that I had mixed emotions. I knew that my mother had lost her mother, and that meant that I could lose my mother. My mother was sad, and nothing seemed to take that sadness away. There was a terrible emptiness in the house that couldn't be filled, and the empty bed and the wheelchair were reminders of that emptiness. At the same time, there was a sense of peace. My mother talked about her faith and God's presence making her strong. Prayer was very much a part of our lives, and it was also a way for us to be together during a difficult time.

I remember thinking that our lives would now return to normal, that sickness would no longer fill our home. Along with sadness, I felt a certain relief. I had yet to forgive my grandmother for her intrusion into our home and for what I saw as her impatience with my mother; this would take time. Over the years, my family expressed gratitude that they had been able to care for my grandmother as she had cared for them, and eventually I felt that gratitude as well. My mother survived her sadness, but there were always tears in her eyes when she talked about those days.

Of course our lifestyles were different then. Nursing homes were not as prevalent, and in some ways there was no choice in the matter. My parents didn't have the "luxury" of asking, "Are the children old enough to attend the wake or the funeral?" Life went on, and part of life was caring for the sick and burying the dead. The way they lived out that experience reflected our belief in the God whose presence allowed us to do more than we thought possible. Saint Paul says in his letter to the people of Ephesus, "Now to him who is able to accomplish far more than all we ask or imagine, by the power at work within us, to him be glory in the church and in Christ Jesus to all generations, forever and ever. Amen" (Eph. 3:20–21). As a child I got the message. Life took on new meaning in the face of death. Whether it was purchasing the grave or attending the funeral Mass, it was not only an end but also a new beginning. My grandmother's dying was very much a part of our living. In the end it touched something very deep in me. God wasn't seen as the one who took my grandmother away; rather, God in Jesus came to be known as the one who gave new life to her in heaven. The wake, the funeral Mass, the prayers, the procession, the incense, the people who came, even sitting in the front bench in the church, gave a sense of belonging to a seven-year-old child that is still with me to this day. Prayer, Scripture, and the sacraments allowed me to probe the mystery further, to forgive my grandmother for her intrusion into our lives, and to be forgiven in return.

As Zachary Hayes points out in *Visions of a Future* (1989), "It has long been a conviction of Christian theology that the human person is, in its deepest reality, a radical openness to the mystery of God. Augustine gave this conviction classical expression when he wrote: 'Thou has made us for Thyself, and our hearts are restless until they rest in Thee.' For Augustine the whole of life appeared to be a search for the truth, goodness, and beauty of reality in the created world. Since created beings are but limited participations in the mystery of being, the desire of the human heart is never stilled by them. No matter how much we may be filled with created goods the dynamism of the human heart impels us beyond them to the mystery of God" (p. 71).

It might have come as a surprise that such a young child would have been so aware of the mystery that was unfolding in our family in those months. But children have a tremendous potential to be open to the mystery of God, and they yearn for God's attributes, goodness, truth, and beauty. My grandmother's suffering and death and my parents' response allowed me to witness firsthand how their beliefs were lived out. The "explanation" went far beyond words and touched the mystery of God's presence in goodness, truth, and beauty even in life's most painful moments. While death affects every child differently and grief will be expressed differently, each child has a spirit that searches for God. In Christ, Catholics are challenged to nurture the spiritual lives of the children "so they may not grieve like the rest who have no hope" (1 Thess. 4:13).

In the *Order of Christian Funerals* (1989), we are told that, through the funeral rites, the Church acts "as a tender mother" commending the dead to God and giving "witness to its own faith in the future resurrection of the baptized with Christ." During the wake, the funeral, and the burial, family, friends, and the Christian community mirror the journey of human life as a pilgrimage to heaven. The Mass is the principal celebration of the Christian funeral, and reading the Word of God focuses our attention on the promises of Christ, made actual in the Eucharist that is celebrated. There are a number of symbols used throughout the funeral rites that serve as reminders of our common life in Christ that is nurtured in the Church. These are most prominent during the funeral Mass. While families may be tempted to focus only on signs and symbols of earthly life, the Church also invites us to pay attention and take comfort from the signs of our spiritual life in Christ. *The Order of Christian Funerals* tells us that the symbols most commonly used are the following:

- the Easter candle: a sign of Christ's undying presence;
- blessed holy water: a sign of the saving waters of baptism;
- incense: a sign of honor to the body of the person who has died, a sign of the community's prayers rising to God, a sign of farewell;
- the liturgical color (usually white): a sign of hope;
- white pall placed on the coffin: a sign of Christian dignity of the person, a reminder of the baptismal garment;
- Bible or book of Gospels placed on the coffin: a sign that faithfulness to the Word of God leads to eternal life;
- cross placed on the coffin: reminds us that the Christian is marked by the cross in baptism.

Writing the family stories about the struggle to explain death to children helped me realize in a new way how compelling those experiences were. The stories stirred memories of suffering, loss, and the grieving process that followed. In retrospect, I see myself as a mother wanting only to respond with tenderness for her child who is struggling with his grief. I remember the discouragement of not finding the right words to explain all that had happened. In looking back, I also see that it is important to acknowledge how real the experience of grieving is for the child and that children and adults are comforted by that faith that gives meaning to their everyday lives. For Catholics, as we struggle to explain death, the Church consistently offers in ritual, in symbol, and in our ongoing life in Christ a witness to its own faith in the future resurrection of the baptized with Christ. This Catholic identity, at times instinctive, offers a frame of reference in the worst of times. For the Catholic, death is an inevitable aspect of a life that is deeply related to our relationship with God in Jesus Christ and lived out through the sacraments, Scriptures, prayer, and our love and care for one another in Christ.

Bibliography

Coles, Robert. 1990. *The Spiritual Life of Children*. Boston: Houghton Mifflin.

Hayes, Zachary. 1989. *Visions of a Future: A Study of Christian Eschatology*. Wilmington: Michael Glazier.

The New American Bible. 1988. Huntington, Ind.: Our Sunday Visitor.

Order of Christian Funerals. 1989. Collegeville, Minn.: Liturgical.

The Rites of the Catholic Church. 1983. New York: Pueblo.

Whitehead, Evelyn, and James Whitehead. 1979. *Christian Life Patterns: The Psychological Challenges and Religious Invitations of Adult Life*. New York: Doubleday.

Explaining Death to Children from Jewish Perspectives

EARL A. GROLLMAN

In Judaism, it is a sacred commandment to comfort mourners—young and old. There is solace and security for children in the knowledge that centuries of tradition lie behind the rituals their parents and grandparents practiced before them. The Jewish faith recognizes the children's confused emotions at this time of great sorrow and helps them through their grief to ease slowly back into the rhythm of life.

Earl A. Grollman, D.D., was the rabbi of the Beth El Temple Center in Belmont, Mass., for thirty-six years. A past president of the Massachusetts Board of Rabbis, he was honored with the Distinguished Service Award from Yeshivah University and an honorary degree from the Hebrew Union College–Jewish Institute of Religion for his pioneering work in the field of crisis intervention.

For people of all ages, death poses the eternal mystery at the core of our most significant philosophical systems of thought. Yet we can prepare children for death and help them to better understand it. It is imperative to explain to the Jewish child the meaning of the ceremonies related to the traditions of death. Do not wait until a death has occurred. Discuss death openly in the home, the religious school, and the synagogue. Discuss the subject at the child's level in an informal atmosphere, always conveying warmth and support as well as belief. Strive to help children develop spiritually and not to convince them that a particular theological doctrine is true. Don't impart a fanciful doctrine that the child will later need to unlearn; adults should test their own beliefs in the light of what they teach. Children, guileless as they may seem, easily sense adults' insincerity. Adults should not indicate that they have the final answers, which a child must simply accept. No one knows God fully or understands the mystery of death. The door must remain open to doubt, questioning, and differences of opinion. Children better develop the capacity to understand the real implications of death when adults are open, loving, and truthful—when death is not associated with guilt, superstition, and unchallenged dogma.

Religion is an experience as well as belief. Children learn what they live. They live what is meaningful to them. In times of crisis, adults are afforded the unique opportunity to offer a more meaningful religion and a more meaningful life to their children.

Rituals: Ceremonies Following Death and Their Meanings for Jewish Children

The basic themes in Jewish mourning rites are *Kevod ha-met*, respect for the person who died, and *Kevod ha-chai*, respect for those who survive. Solomon ben Isaac (known as Rashi), an eleventh-century commentator on the Bible, explains the origins of *Kevod ha-met*. In Genesis 4:27, the elderly Patriarch Jacob asked his son, Joseph, to arrange a burial for him in the land of Israel. Joseph's fulfillment of this request, this act of caring for the dead (*Kevod ha-met*), was the greatest display of kindness. There is no anticipation of reward. In the *Ethics of The Fathers* (1:3), Antigonos of Socho writes, "Be like servants who serve the

Masters without the expectation of receiving a reward." Similarly, there is an entire section of the Talmud (*semachot*) in which God comforts and consoles those in the midst of suffering and despair, illustrating the dictate of *Kevod ha-chai*, respect for the mourners.

Many of the traditional customs pertaining to death are presented in the *Code of Jewish Law* (*Shulchan Aruch*) prepared by Joseph Caro in 1565 in Venice. Yet there are wide variations and practices within Jewish life.

When informed of the death, the family may recite together the prayer, "Baruch atah adonai elohenu melech ha-olam dayan ha-emet" (Blessed is the Lord, our God, Ruler of the Universe, Judge of Truth), an affirmation of faith and acceptance of the reality of death.

Following the death of a loved one, Jewish law (*Halacha*) prescribes periods of mourning. The specific length of time between death and burial is known in Hebrew as *aninut*. The mourners, whether *anen* (literally, a male who is distressed) or *anenut* (a female), are defined as the nearest of kin (Lev. 21:1–3); they are exempt from all ritual and social obligations, with the sole exceptions of Sabbath observance and the arrangement of the funeral and burial. Minors (boys younger than thirteen and girls younger than twelve) are traditionally relieved from the laws of mourning. Nevertheless, there is nothing in Jewish law that proscribes a child's participation in the mourning rituals. Since one of the worst problems in children's lack of understanding is adult secrecy and exclusion, rabbis today believe that young people should be encouraged to express their sorrow through the Jewish ceremonies of death—always sensitive to the child's age, comprehension, and desire for involvement.

Jewish law (Deut. 21:23) insists that the funeral take place as soon as possible. Visitation before the service is not in keeping with Jewish tradition. In order to allow families and friends from distant places to attend, the funeral is generally conducted within a few days of death rather than on the same day. During this period, children may wish to be with their peers and receive comfort from their friends.

Children may ask, "Now that the person has died, what happens to the body?" The loved one is most often released by the family to a funeral director or *Chevra Kedusha* (communal burial society) for preparation according to Jewish practice. There may be *Tahara* (meaning "to purify"), where the body is washed and dressed in order to return in a state of purity. There may be a *Shomer* (male "guardian" or "watcher"; feminine, *Shomeret*) who stays with the body until burial and reads from Scripture, usually Psalms 23, 91, and 119. According to the Talmud (*Berakoth* 18A), the body is guarded to prevent mutilation by roving beasts. In Jewish history, there are accounts of vicious anti-Semites who snatched dead bodies, and the *Shomer* literally became "a guard."

Public viewing of the body and cosmeticization of the body is against Jewish law (there is no equivalent of the Christian "wake"). The rabbis urge that we remember the dead as they were in life. However, the family may desire to view the body privately before the funeral begins since the casket is permanently sealed before the service. Embalming is prohibited in traditional Judaism except when government regulations require it or when the body is to be transported a long distance for burial. There are branches of Judaism that emphasize the overriding principle of *pikkuach nefesh*, the saving of the lives of the living, and therefore encourage organ donation so that death serves life.

Flowers are discouraged, and charitable donations are often given to a hospice, hospital, synagogue, or research foundation instead.

At the service, the entire family—including children—performs *Keria* (which means "tear"). This practice derives from Genesis; when Jacob believed that his son, Joseph, was killed, the father "rent his garments" (37:34). Today, many mourners indicate their anguish by cutting a black ribbon, usually at the funeral chapel or at the cemetery prior to interment. The ceremony is performed standing up to teach the bereaved to "meet all sorrow standing upright." Instead of a ribbon, traditional Jews may tear a coat or a dress. The torn garment or black ribbon is usually worn after the funeral for seven days, or, for some, thirty days. Mourners perform *Keria* on the left side for a parent and on the right side for other members of the family. The torn ribbon or clothing is not worn on the Sabbath or major Jewish holidays.

The loved one may be buried in ordinary clothes. Adult males usually wear a talit (a prayer shawl) and a yarmelka (a head covering). Others are buried in plain shrouds (Hebrew, *Tachrichim*) to emphasize equality in death, for there are no pockets in shrouds. Says the *Ethics of the Fathers* (16:9), "When we die, it is neither silver nor gold nor gems nor pearls that accompany us, only Torah [learning] and good deeds."

Jewish law requires that the casket be made of wood without metal nails because metal slows the natural process of decomposition: "Dust you are and to dust you shall return" (Gen. 3:19). Simplicity and lack of ostentation are the governing principles of casket selection.

Years ago, most Jewish funerals were held in the home, except for great scholars, whose services were conducted in the synagogue. Today, most funerals are conducted at a funeral home, a synagogue, a cemetery chapel, or the grave side. Funerals are held during the day and not on the Sabbath (Saturday) or major Jewish holidays.

Since the natural decomposition of the body is required, cremation is contrary to Jewish law. However, the practice is permitted in Reform and Reconstructionist Judaism, as long as a funeral is held with the body present. Even though, in ancient times, bodies were buried in mausoleums, caves, and tombs, earth burial is the most accepted form of internment.

A public funeral affords members of the community of all ages an opportunity to offer support and share sorrow. All the emotional reactions that the bereaved are likely to experience—sorrow and loneliness, anger and rejection, guilt, anxiety about the future, and the conviction that nothing is certain or stable anymore—can be lessened by the support of caring friends. Jews and non-Jews alike are welcome.

At the funeral, the rabbi recites those prayers that are expressive of both the spirit of Judaism and the memory of the deceased. The most commonly used text, Psalm 23, expresses the faith of the members of the flock in the justice of the Divine Shepherd. From the Psalm "O Lord, what is man?" we hear that, although "our days are a passing shadow," there is immortality for those who have "treasured their days with a heart of wisdom." During the recitation of the prayer *El Molay Rachamim*, the name of the loved one is mentioned. The eulogy of the dead (*Hesped*) is included in the service to recognize not only that a death has occurred but also that a life has been lived.

Kevod ha-met means to bring reverence and dignity to the one who has died. Like other members of the household, children should have the privilege of expressing their love and devotion. Participation aids them in understanding the finality of death and dispelling their fantasies. If they are old enough to attend a synagogue and comprehend in part what is taking place, they should be allowed to attend a religious ceremony to say *L'Hitraot* (farewell) or *Shalom* (peace) to a significant person in their lives.

In Judaism, accompanying the dead to the grave (*Halavayat ha-met*) is considered the highest form of loving kindness (*Hessed shel emet*). The funeral ends, not in the chapel, but after the dead person has been accompanied to the final burial place. Witnessing the burial (*K'vurah*) may help teach children the importance of leave-taking and give them basic emotional tools for dealing with unfinished feelings. An expression of consolation recited by friends as the mourners leave the grave is the Hebrew "Ha-Makom Yinachem Et-Chem B'toch Sh'ar A-Vay-Lay Tzion Virushalaymim" (May God comfort you along with all the mourners of Zion and Jerusalem). *Shivah* (meaning "seven") consists of the seven days of mourning when most family members remain at home and refrain from their ordinary pursuits and occupations. Children may go back to school for some of the period if both parents and child together make this decision.

In returning to the *Beit Avel* (the mourners' home), some may wash their hands, which according to Rabbi Isaac Klein "symbolically indicates that our hands are clean of death; we did everything to help this person live or to ease his/her pain" (1975, 18).

Immediately on returning from the cemetery, a light (*Shiva* candle) is kindled and remains burning for the entire seven days of mourning. Before his death, the great sage Judah Ha-Nasi, the third-century editor of the Talmud, instructed that a light should be kept aflame in his home: "Light is the symbol of the divine. The Lord is my light and my salvation."

The practice of covering mirrors is not based on explicit Jewish law. Some authorities regard this practice as superstitious and discourage its use. Others interpret the rite symbolically to mean that we ought not to gaze on our reflection in the mirror of the house of mourning for, in so doing, we appear to be reflecting on ourselves.

During the week, the community reaches out to both adult and child. Friends demonstrate their concern and love. The first food (*Seu-*

dat havra-ah) is traditionally prepared by others. Jewish tradition creates a sense of belonging, of solidarity, of cohesiveness. Even though minors are exempt from many of the mourning rites, they are permitted and encouraged to participate in these significant family ceremonies. They are given the opportunity to help and be helped. And, by their very presence, they may help the bereft adult who questions, "Why should I go on living?"

During *Shiva*, religious services may be observed in the mourners' home. The bereaved recite the *Kaddish* prayer ("May God's name be magnified and exalted"), a pledge of rededication to the God of Life. They belong to the largest company in the world—the company of those who have known anguish and death. The great, universal sense of sorrow helps unite human hearts and dissolve all other feelings into those of common sympathy and understanding.

Sheloshim (meaning "thirty") is the thirty-day period after death. During *Sheloshim*, life gradually returns to normal for the mourners, but they will avoid joyful social events. (Children need not observe the same aspects of bereavement.) For most mourners, *Sheloshim* concludes the period of bereavement but, for those whose parents have died, mourning concludes twelve months from the day of the death.

The anniversary of the death (*Yahrzeit*) is observed annually on the date of death, commencing on the preceding day and concluding on the anniversary day at sunset. *Kaddish* is recited in the synagogue, and a *Yahrzeit* candle is kindled.

The service of commemoration of the tombstone or plaque is called the "unveiling." The time of the unveiling may be any time after *Sheloshim* and usually before the first year of mourning is over. Unveilings are not held on the Sabbath or on festivals. Any member of the family or a close friend may intone the appropriate prayers, usually a few psalms, the *El Molay Rachamim* ("God, full of compassion"), and the *Kaddish*. Visitation at the grave may be made as often as one wishes following the initial thirty-day period.

The memorial prayer of *Yizkor* ("May God *remember* the soul of my revered") is said four times a year during the synagogue worship; on the holidays of *Yom Kippur*, *Shemini Atzeret*, *Pesach*, and *Shavuot*. It is not recited during the first year of mourning.

Jewish rituals are community rituals. They are performed by those who share a religious sameness. Tradition creates a sense of solidarity, of belonging, the feeling that one is a member of the group, with all the comfort and gratification that such a cohesiveness brings.

The Jewish faith holds it as desirable that with time the havoc wrought by death should help repair itself. Although they are never the same after the death, when mourning is over, the bereaved are expected to take up existence for the sake of life itself. The garment (*Kena*) that pious mourners rend can be sewn and worn again. The scar is there, but life must resume its course. Jewish mourning helps the mourner face reality, show respect for the person who died, and receive help from friends and family during the period of sadness and grief. When sadness comes, neither children nor adults need to walk the lonely road alone.

Beliefs: Meanings of Death in Jewish Life

Jewish people pray to the God of Abraham, God of Isaac, God of Jacob, God of Sarah, God of Rebekah, God of Leah, and God of Rachel. The God of each is the same God. Each person has to find God in his or her own way. Similarly, there are many Jewish concepts of death. Judaism has no dogmatic creed. During the course of the centuries, many ideas have been presented.

The great scholar George F. Moore enumerated the many theories about death in Jewish literature and stated, "Any attempt to systematize the Jewish notions of the hereafter imposes upon them an order and consistency which does not exist in them" (1954, 2:380). This split began in the beginning of the first Christian century, when the party of the Sadducees rejected a belief in an afterlife, while the Pharisees did not.

Judaism has not wholly harmonized or integrated a precept of death and the hereafter. However, in spite of the varied beliefs maintained throughout its history, there are central and unifying patterns. Here, I outline these patterns and describe how they can be explained to children in age-appropriate ways.

Death Is Real and Inescapable

Being part of God's process of birth, growth, and decay, no form of existence can escape the democracy of death: "As for man, his days are as grass; as a flower in the field, so he flourisheth. For as the wind persists over it, it is gone; and the place thereof shall know it no more" (Ps. 103:15–16). "For what person can live and never see death?" (Ps. 89:48).

Explain the mystery of death to children as part of the cycle of nature. Trees and plants may die, but look, other shoots are beginning to come up. Nature constantly renews itself. Living and dying are part of human unfolding. There are the cyclic rhythms of nature—night and day, phases of the moon, seasons, lives of insects, plants, animals, and people.

Dead Bodies No Longer Function

Death is the annihilation of life—the rupture of pleasures with family and friends: "There is no work or thought" (Eccles. 9:10). "There is no remembrance of Thee" (Ps. 115:17). "The dead have no more forever any share in all that is done under the sun" (Eccles. 9:6).

In my *Talking about Death* (1990), I explained this concept in these words: "But what does death mean? Remember when we saw the animal that was hit by the car. It was lying on the road . . . still . . . not breathing . . . not moving . . . its heart wasn't beating anymore. The animal would never breathe or move again. It was dead. It's the same for people. The body doesn't move. It doesn't breathe. The heart doesn't beat. The body is still . . . quiet and peaceful. There is no hurt, no pain, no life" (1990, 15).

Focus on Life and Living

"Better is one hour of repentance and good deeds in this world than the whole life of the world-to-come" (*Ethics of the Fathers* 4:17).

In the face of death, Judaism affirms life. The Hebrew Bible tells of the time when a first child was born to Bathsheba and David. The child was critically ill. David spent the whole night in deep prayer, refusing to eat, for he was prostrate with apprehension. Shortly, the infant died. The servants were afraid to tell David of the sad news. But David sensed from their behavior that the child was no longer living. As soon as his fears were confirmed, he rose from the earth, washed himself, worshiped, then ate. His servants were puzzled over the strange contrast between his behavior before and after the child's death. David explained as follows: "While the child was yet alive, I fasted and wept; for I said, 'Who knoweth whether the Lord will not be gracious to me, that the child may live?' But now that he is dead, wherefore should I fast? Can I bring him back again?" (2 Sam. 12:15–23).

When David himself died, his son Solomon posed this dilemma to the authorities: "My father is dead and lying in the sun, and my father's dogs are hungry. What shall I do?" The authorities answered, "Feed the dogs first, then take care of your father's body" (1 Kings 2:1–12). This answer indicates, not an insensitivity to the anguish of death, but an affirmation of life.

Children as well as adults participate in *Keria*, the cutting of the ribbon or garment standing upright. Even in suffering, the emphasis is *L'Chayim*—to life. Life is for the living.

Memories Never Die

Death is not the end of life—not just because there might be an afterlife, but because the deceased's ideals and influence will continue to shape the people he or she has known. The ancient Egyptians buried their dead with all the things a living person needs, such as clothes, weapons, and food, and were more preoccupied with death than with life. In contrast, Louis Ginzberg noted that the Jews fixed the center of gravity not in a world beyond but rather to foster and establish it in the actual life of man of earth. The memorial prayer, *Yizkor*, means always to remember those who walked before us in order that their memory may bring strength and blessing.

Share with children memories of time spent with their loved one and how enriched they are now because that person lived. Look through photo albums and recall happy moments. Consider whether a personal possession of the one who died might become a treasured memento for the child.

Jewish Meanings of Life after Death

Moses Maimonides, one of the great Jewish philosophers, asserted that, when we discuss the subject of death, we are like blind people attempting to understand the nature of light. How much more so this is for children. Explanations to children should especially be in simple

Explaining Death from Jewish Perspectives

words or stories. In the words of the Hebrew book *Ben Sira* (the Latin title is *Ecclesiasticus*), "Do not inquire what is beyond thine understanding" (Eccles. 42:21).

There is no universal Jewish theology of death, but I mention some of the general concepts here in order that adults and children may join in the dialogue of ideas.

Justice in Death

Unfortunately, many lives are not merciful and just. Should there not be rewards for the righteous as well as penalties for evildoers? Each is reminded that he or she must give an account to the Eternal Judge: "None will escape his punishment and no virtue will be unrewarded" (*Ethics of The Fathers* 4:16–17).

Jews may find comfort in the belief that, however difficult a person's life, in the hereafter the crooked will be straight and each will be given according to his or her deserts. The scale of cosmic equity will create equal justice.

The Immortal Soul

In Judaism, before the body comes into being, the soul already exists. It is pure and untainted by original sin. Every morning the devout Jew prays, "O my God, the soul which Thou gave me is pure." The exact place of the soul is not determined. This is another of the mysteries of life.

Often, in their struggle to understand death, children will ask such questions as, "What happens to us after we die? Are we dead and gone forever?" Perhaps their questions can best be answered by drawing a parallel in story form:

A little boy once found a bird's nest near his home that contained speckled eggs. Fascinated, he watched it for a long time until he had to take a trip to the city. On his return, he rushed to the nest to see the eggs. He was shocked to find that the beautiful eggs were broken. All he saw were empty shells. He wept before his father, "These beautiful eggs are spoiled and broken." "No, my son," answered his father. "They're not spoiled. All you see is the empty shell. The birds have escaped from the eggs, and soon they will be flying around in the sky.

This is the way nature intended it to be. And so it is when we die. Our souls leave our bodies. All that's left is the empty shell."

"But," asked the lad, "how do you know that we have a soul? You can't see it or touch it. How do you know?"

The parent replied, "We don't have visible proof, but many people have faith that it is so. They believe that the soul is that part of God in us that lives on forever. And no part of God can be destroyed.

"When we believe in something very much without being able to prove it, that is faith. When Columbus set out on his first voyage from the shores of Spain, he was not sure what was beyond the vision of his eye, but he had faith that the great sea had another shore. So we cannot see beyond this life, but many believe that the soul continues. You can trust in God!"

A belief in the immortality of the soul is an accepted doctrine in most branches of Judaism.

The Soul Is Reunited with the Body

The earlier history of Israel was predominantly concerned with the survival of nationhood. Theologically, rewards and punishment related to the community rather than the individual. In the fourth pre-Christian century, with the physical conquest of Palestine and the intellectual influence of the Greeks, the doctrine of resurrection became prevalent. (There are isolated references earlier in the Hebrew Bible.)

Resurrection, the reunion of body and soul, is called in Hebrew *Teh-iyyath Hamathem*. The dead would rise and stand in judgment before God in the Messianic age. The exact nature of the Messiah is unclear. Biblically, the concept is related to a period of time, "the end of days" (Isa. 2:2–4) in a world of peace and justice for all humankind. Later, in the second Christian century, the belief in a Messiah focused on an actual person, a descendant of King David who would be heralded by the blast of the shafar, the ram's horn. God would pronounce a judgment of damnation or bliss in the *olam haba*, the world to come. Traditional Jews pray in the grace after meals, "May the All Merciful make us worthy of the days of the Messiah and the world to come."

Most Reform, Reconstructionist, and some Conservative rabbis do not adhere to the belief in the physical resurrection of the dead. Many additional references are deleted from the prayer books and, when inserted, are regarded poetically rather than literally.

Within Jewish movements, there is the widest possible latitude for differences of opinion. There are many thoughts, yet none is declared authoritative and final. The tradition teaches but, at the same time, seems to say that there is much that we do not know and still more that we have to learn. And, even then, only God can completely discern the mysteries of life and death.

Despite the diversity of theological beliefs and ritual practices, Judaism helps its adherents face death and face away from it. It aids them to accept the reality of death and protects them from destructive fantasy and illusion in the denial of fact. Most important of all, the Jewish religion offers an abundance of shared religious resources in the encounter with helplessness, guilt, loneliness, and fear. Although reason cannot answer the *why* and comforting words cannot wipe away tears, Judaism offers consolation in death by reaffirming life with ceremonials and beliefs, with tears and stories, with food and friends, with memories and a "love that is as strong as death. For many waters cannot quench love, neither can the floods drown it" (*Song of Songs* 8:7).

Glossary

Avelim (pron. ah-veh-leem), lit. "mourners." Laws of mourning apply in case of death of seven relatives: father, mother, husband, wife, son or daughter, brother, and sister.

Beit Avel (pron. bate ah-vel), lit. "home of mourner." Where memorial week may be observed.

Ben Sirach, Joshua (third century B.C.E.). Author of ancient book *The Wisdom of Jesus the Son of Sirach*, or *Ecclesiasticus* (Latin title).

Chevra Kedusha (pron. chev-rah ka-dee-shaw), lit. "holy brotherhood." Society whose members devote themselves to burial and rites connected with it.

El Moleh Rachamin (pron. ale moh-lay ra-cha-meen), lit. "God full of compassion." Memorial prayer recited at funerals that dates from the seventeenth century. Popular Yiddish name is *Molay*.

Ethics of the Fathers (Heb. *Pirke Avot*, pron. peer-kay avote) Selected ethical wisdom by the teachers of the *Mishna*.

Gamara (pron. ge-moh-ra). Aramaic commentaries on the Hebrew Bible and on elaboration of the *Mishna* completed in the sixth Christian century.

Ginzberg, Louis (1873–1953). Famous Talmudic scholar and leading contributor to *Jewish Encyclopedia.*

Halacha (pron. hal–la–cha), lit. "the law." Jewish legal decisions as defined by Talmudic and other great scholars.

Hesped (pron. hes–peed). Eulogy delivered by rabbi for deceased. Orations date back to biblical times. Contains an account of life accomplishments of the departed.

Kabbala (pron. kah–bah–lah), lit. "tradition." Applied to important complex of Jewish mystical philosophy and practice. Basic work is *Zohar* (splendor), which appeared at end of thirteenth century.

Kaddish (pron. kah–dish), lit. "holy" or "sanctification." Aramaic prayer for the dead. Essentially a doxology, praising God and praying for speedy establishment of God's kingdom on earth. Recited by mourners for period of eleven months from date of burial.

Keria (pron. ka–ree–ah), lit. "rending." Custom of mourner tearing a section of his or her garment or a black ribbon as symbol of grief. Rite performed before funeral. Rent often made over the left side, over the heart. To be performed standing up, for the mourner is to meet sorrow standing upright.

Kevod ha-chai (pron. kee–vode hah–chaye), lit. "honor the living." Respect for the living survivors.

Kevod ha-met (pron. kee–vode hah–mate), lit. "honor the dead." Respect for the one who died.

Maimonides, Moses (1135–1204). Greatest Jewish philosopher and codifier of the Middle Ages.

Matzevah (pron. mah–tzave–vah). Tombstone that is erected toward the end of the first year of interment.

Midrash (pron. mid–rahsh), lit. "exposition." Books devoted to biblical interpretations. In form of homiletic expositions, legends, and folklore.

Minyan (pron. mean–yahn), lit. "number" or "quorum." Minimum number of ten adults above the age of thirteen required for public services. According to Jewish law, *Minyan* is required for community recital of the *Kaddish.*

Mishna (pron. meesh–nah), lit. "learning." Hebrew interpretations of biblical law written by many scholars, including the third-Christian-century period.

Moore, George Foot (1851–1931). Eminent non-Jewish biblical scholar who wrote the monumental *Judaism in the First Centuries of the Christian Era.*

Olam haba (pron. oh–lam ha–baw), lit. "World to come." Maimonides explains: "The wise men call it world to come not because it is not in existence at present, but because life in that world will come to man after the life in this world is ended."

Pharisees (pron. fair-a-sees). Jewish religious and political party during the Second Temple period.

Rabbi. Leader and teacher in the congregation. Conducts the funeral service, answers many ritual questions regarding the ceremony of death, and aids in important approach of *Mena-chem Avel* (pron. mine-a-chem ah-vel), comforting the bereaved.

Sadducees (pron. sad-u-sees). Major sect among Palestinian Jews during the period of the Second Commonwealth.

Seudat havra-ah (pron. soo-dat chah-vey-rah). Meal of consolation. Provided by friends in accordance with Talmudic injunction. "A mourner is forbidden to eat of his own food at the first meal after the burial."

Sheloshim (pron. sh-lo-sheem), lit. "thirty." Mourning begins on first day of the funeral and ends on morning of the thirtieth day.

Shivah (pron. shee-vah), lit. "seven." Refers to the first seven days of mourning after burial.

Tachrichim (pron. tach-re-cheem), lit. "shroud." Robe in which some dead are buried. Made of white linen cloth.

Tahara (pron. tah-ha-raw), lit. "purity." Ritual of washing and dressing a body prior to the funeral.

Talmud (pron. tahl-mude). Discussions on the text of the *Mishna* by the Palestinian and Babylonian scholars from the third to the fifth century.

Tzedekah (pron. zee-dak-ka), lit. "righteousness." In place of flowers, a charitable contribution is given in memory of a loved one.

Tehiyyath Hamathem (pron. th-chee-yaht ha-may-teem). Resurrection of the dead. Belief that, at end of time, the bodies of dead will rise from the grave.

Unveiling. Tombstone consecration in which special prayers are recited, such as *El Moleh Rachamin* and the mourner's *Kaddish.* It is customary to cover the tombstone with a veil and, during service, for one of the mourners to unveil the stone or plaque.

Yahrzeit (pron. yohr-tzite). Yiddish term for the anniversary of death. Observed by reciting the *Kaddish* in the synagogue and lighting memorial light in home.

Yahrzeit light. Well-established practice of having candle or special lamp in house of mourning for twenty-four hours on the anniversary of death.

Yizkor (pron. yiz-kohr). Prayer, "May God remember the soul of my revered. . . ." Recited on *Yom Kippur, Shemini Atzeret,* last day of *Passover,* and second day of *Shavuot.*

156

BEREAVED CHILDREN AND TEENS

For Further Reading

Coalition for the Advancement of Jewish Education, with the assistance of the
Jewish Funeral Directors of America. 1993. *The Chain of Life: A Curricula
Guide for Teaching about Death, Bereavement, and the Jewish Way of Honoring
the Dead*. New York.

Danby, Herbert. 1933. *The Mishna*. Oxford: Clarendon.

Doka, Kenneth, and John D. Morgan. 1993. *Death and Spirituality*. Amityville, N.Y.: Baywood.

Encyclopedia Judaica. 1971. 17 vols. Jerusalem: Keter.

Fackenheim, Emil L. 1987. *What Is Judaism?* New York: Summit.

Freehof, Solomon B. 1974. *Contemporary Reform Responsa*. Cincinnati: Hebrew Union College Press.

Gates of Prayer. 1975. New York: Central Conference of America's Rabbis.

Ginzberg, Louis. 1956. *The Legends of the Jews*. 7 vols. Philadelphia: Jewish
Publication Society.

Goldberg, Chayim Binyamin. 1991. *Mourning in Halachah*. New York:
Mesorah.

Grollman, Earl A. 1990. *Talking about Death: A Dialogue between Parent and
Child*. Boston: Beacon.

Grollman, Sharon H. 1988. *Shira: A Legacy of Courage*. New York: Doubleday.

The Holy Scriptures. 1917. Philadelphia: Jewish Publication Society of
America.

Isaacs, Ronald H. 1992. *Rites of Passage: A Jewish Guide to the Jewish Life Cycle*.
Hoboken, NJ: KTAV.

Kay, Alan A. 1993. *The Jewish Book of Comfort for Mourners*. Northwalk,
N.J.: Aronson.

Klein, Isaac. 1975. *Responsa and Halachic Studies*. New York: KTAC.

Kolatch, Alfred J. 1993. *The Jewish Mourner's Book of Why*. New York: Jona-
than David.

Lamm, Maurice. 1969. *The Jewish Way in Death and Mourning*. New York: Jon-
athan David.

Moore, George Foot. 1954. *Judaism*. 3 vols. Cambridge, MA: Harvard University Press.

Olitzky, Kerry M., ed. 1993. *When Your Jewish Child Asks Why?* Hoboken,
NJ: KTAV.

Riemer, Jack. 1974. *Jewish Reflections on Death*. New York: Schocken.

Sonsino, Rifat, and Daniel B. Syme. 1990. *What Happens after I Die?* New
York: Union of American Hebrew Congregations.

Syme, Daniel B. 1989. *Jewish Mourning*. New York: Union of American Hebrew Congregations.

Techner, David, and Judith Hirt-Manheimer. 1993. *A Candle for Grandpa*. New York: Union of American Hebrew Congregations.

Weiss, Abner. 1991. *Death and Bereavement: A Halakhic Guide*. Hoboken, NJ: KTAV.

Zlotnick, Dov. 1966. *The Tractate Mourning (Semachot)*. New Haven, CT: Yale University Press.

A Philosopher Looks at Children and Death

JOHN D. MORGAN

The subject of death and children has been discussed from many perspectives: by the sociologist from the social environment; by the psychologist from the personal context; by the anthropologist from the cultural realm; and by the religionist from the faith community. All have attempted to respond to the pressing need for dialogue. Until now, the philosophical view has been sadly neglected. "Lovers of wisdom"—René Descartes, William James, Phillipe Ariès, Ernest Becker, and others—have much to offer in helping confront the topic of explaining death to children.

John D. Morgan, Ph.D., is professor of philosophy at King's College of the University of Western Ontario, London, Ontario. For more than thirteen years he has been coordinator of death education at that institution, where thousands of professionals from around the world convene for the International Conference on Death, Dying, and Bereavement. He is the senior editor of many volumes of Death, Value, and Meaning *for the Baywood Publishing Company.*

The confrontation of the ideas of *children* and *death* challenges our basic understandings of life, death, and God. In this chapter, I examine the meaning of death in our lives and show what the juxtaposition of children and death does to our attitudes about life and death.

What Philosophy Is

The word *philosophy* has its roots in the Greek words *philos* and *sophia*, which are usually translated as "the love of wisdom." In Western culture, we name Thales in the seventh century B.C.E. as the first philosopher because he was the first person to have answered fundamental questions about the nature of human experience without appealing either to traditional knowledge or to religion. Thales and his successors were called philosophers because they would not easily accept either the everyday answers of common sense or the explanations of mythology.[1]

Philosophy is a rational enterprise. The term *rational* is ambiguous because it has at least two different meanings. One of them refers to the ideas of the seventeenth-century thinker René Descartes and his followers.

According to Descartes, at least some knowledge—rational knowledge—can be attained simply through thought, independent of experience.[2] A more basic meaning of *rationalism*, the one with which persons outside philosophy would be comfortable, is "the view which affirms reason, with its interest in evidence, examination, and evaluation, as authoritative in all matters of belief and conduct."[3] Philosophy is rational in this latter sense because it uses reason and evidence as the sole or chief criterion of one's convictions.

Philosophy differs both from religion and from the natural and social sciences because these disciplines have presuppositions that are commonly, if not universally, accepted. For example, Jewish, Christian, and Islamic thinkers accept the belief that God has revealed certain truths to humankind as fundamental.[4] Similarly, chemistry, physics, and other natural sciences presuppose the existence of a physical world that operates in predictable, orderly ways,[5] and psychology, sociology, and other social sciences assume that human persons exist, that they form groups, and that they learn and act in knowable, predictable ways.[6] Philosophical reflection, however, is different because even its presuppositions are open to rational critique.

The Rational World

Humans are not born with innate ideas, but some insights are so fundamental to the way the human mind operates that we learn them early in our lives. The principle of sufficient reason is one of these. This principle states that there is a reason for whatever happens. This is not to say that there is a morally, pedagogically, or economically sufficient reason for whatever happens, or even an otherwise *good* reason. But the principle does claim that *nothing does nothing*; therefore, *if something happens, there must be a reason for that happening.* This principle is, in reality, the foundation of all logical thinking. It cannot, of course, be proved since it is the foundation of all proof; that is, all proof assumes that there is a reason for the conclusion in the premises.

In communication, a speaker expresses the content of his or her mind through the medium of words in such a manner that another person, the hearer, is able to use those words to understand the content of the speaker's mind. This communication of ideas is possible only because the human mind is capable of abstracting from day-to-day immediate experience the common elements of experience and can convert those common elements, or ideas, into words that can be received by another. The fact of communication implies that the human mind is able to draw from experience the basic characteristics of things. This understanding of the characteristics of things is precisely what is meant by *thinking.*[7] Not only are we able to abstract universal characteristics, but we are also able to formulate them into hypotheses or laws.

The Natural Law

As we comprehend the characteristics of things, we become aware of their uniformity of behavior. The sun rises and sets; one season follows on another; water freezes and boils in a consistent manner. This consistency of order in the universe has been called *natural law.* If we believe that the physical, chemical, and biological world is directed to the good of the human race, then that understanding implies a divine lawgiver who has concern for the good of the universe and especially the persons in it.[8]

While many philosophers, today and throughout the history of thought, would disagree with my analysis, the overwhelming number of thinkers would agree that the universe is a reasonable place because it was created by a reasonable lawgiver who has created the universe for the benefit of human persons.

A Death Attitude System

Death is a biological fact. Bereavement—the loss of a person important to us—is a psychological fact. But, while death and bereavement are *facts*, dying and grief are *processes* in which we engage according to our attitudes. Like the other attitudes we have, our attitudes about death, dying, and bereavement are not innate; they were taught to us by our culture. The set of attitudes by which we live our dying and grieving has been called a *death system*[9]—a cognitive, affective, and behavioral orientation toward death that teaches us what to think about death, how to feel about it, and what to do with reference to it.

Different cultures have different ways of looking at death, dying, and bereavement. In some cultures, death is seen primarily as a familiar friend, in others as primarily the loss of a relationship, and in still others primarily as the end of a personal journey.[10] In addition to varying across cultures, death attitudes also change over time. Death attitudes differ and have changed because of differences and changes in four major factors—*life expectancy, exposure to death, perceived control over the forces of nature*, and *the understanding of what it is to be a human person*.

In areas where life expectancy is high, it is possible for children to have little or even no personal exposure to the death of a significant other until age twenty or thirty. There are many places in the world where this "innocence of death" is not the case. Our ancestors had a different understanding of the fragility of life. They often viewed death as a neighbor, if not always a welcome one. In the war-, starvation-, and violence-torn places on the globe today, children grow up with the realization that persons die, and often die young. The amount of experience one has with death will shape one's death attitudes profoundly.

More fundamentally, our attitudes toward death are shaped by our philosophy, our views about the world, and our place in it. If we believe that we are impotently subject to the laws of nature, then our death attitudes will differ from those who think that we have significant control over the forces of nature. Those who live in the floodplain of Bangladesh, the slums of Mexico City, or shadow of Mount Pinatubo have a different perception of their control over the forces of nature than do those of us who move about or reside in climate-controlled cars, offices, and homes. If we believe that we can be protected from nature, then we have less respect for the power of nature over life.

In a culture such as that of the United States or Canada, which puts its emphasis on the uniqueness of the individual and individual rights, persons will have a different orientation toward death than in a culture that perceives each individual as having meaning primarily as part of a religious or political whole or as having no meaning at all. It would be a mistake to assume that every culture places the same value on individual uniqueness. Those who believe that each life is unique will perceive the end of that life as a different order of loss than those who perceive that a life has meaning only within a whole.

Death Ignored

Death today is more technological, isolating, and ambiguous than it has been in the past. We now have "clinical death" and "brain death," and only doctors can certify that such a death has occurred. In earlier days, the physician's primary role was to be with the sick, to encourage the body's own recuperative powers to regenerate, and, as Paul Ramsey stated, "to (only) care for the dying."[11] Today, doctors deal as much with drugs and machines as with people, and care of the dying has moved from the home to the hospital; the result is that the process of dying is seen by fewer people. In prolonging life, medical technology separated the chronically ill and the dying from their families.

Although death rates have improved in the population as a whole over the past century, the benefits have not been shared equally. Women outlive men as they always have. The age-adjusted mortality rate, which fell 26 percent for elderly males between 1940 and 1980, dropped 48 percent for elderly females at the same time.[12] In the cases of people with relatively similar lifestyles, such as a monastery of men and a convent of women, both leading lives of quiet prayer, the women still outlive the men.[13] There are other examples of death discrimination. Race, poverty, and poor education are predictors of early death. The mortality rate from heart disease in 1986 for blacks was 1.3 times higher than that for whites.[14] From 1983 to 1988, the percentage of individuals with an annual income over $60,000 whose activity was limited owing to a chronic condition declined, while for those with lower incomes the figures actually increased.[15] The poor and dispossessed are much more conscious of the place of death in their lives than are white, middle- and upper-class North Americans. One of the tragedies of our death awareness is that, while most women will outlive their husbands, few women consciously prepare for this eventuality.

Perhaps the greatest single element in the formation of our attitudes toward death is the perception of the *person as unique*. In the Western world today, we are seemingly more conscious of our individuality than in other parts of the world and other historical eras. We believe that there is a self hidden within each of us that no list of characteristics captures, what Becker refers to as "the ache of cosmic specialness."[16] The dominant philosophy of education is existentialism, with its stress on feeling good about oneself.[17]

The effect of an increased life span and a lessened exposure to death is a lowered consciousness of and respect for the power of death. We know that death exists. Our lifetime has seen more deaths than the entire previous history of the human race. We have lived in the shadow of the Holocaust and of nuclear destruction. We accept the abstraction of even our own death. Indeed, the evidence is that college students think about death more often than did their grandparents.[18] But we do not have an *affective consciousness* of death. We do not seem to accept the *real probability* of death, much less its *appropriateness*.

A Philosopher Looks at Children and Death

William James has said that the word *good* fundamentally means "destined to survive."[19] When an individual says that something is good, he or she implicitly affirms that the thing ought to exist. The effect of self-awareness is the following enigma. *I am. I am good. Yet I shall die.* In the words of William James, this awareness is "the worm at the core of our pretensions to happiness."[20] We do not seem to take seriously that death is the end of our possibilities.[21] As death is removed from daily consciousness, it appears to be *less appropriate*, creating more complicated grief.[22] Philippe Ariès calls our orientation "death denied."[23]

There are many effects of our ignoring or denial of death. There is substantial evidence that the violence that grows daily as well as addiction and poverty are results of our refusal to take seriously the human reality of death.[24] Not taking death seriously allows us to risk the lives of others, our loved ones, and ourselves. According to Ernest Becker, violence is "a symbolic solution of a biological limitation." It is easy to believe that one is master of one's own life when one holds someone else's fate in one's hands.[25] In order to feel more in control of one's own fate, one takes action against those who are viewed as a threat.[26]

Children and Death

The Death of Children

As I have shown above, our basic philosophical orientation is that we live in a predictable world. We believe that the universe is governed by God for our benefit. However, there are two flaws in this model. First of all, only a limited part of the human experience can be thought of as orderly. In particular, death is not evenly distributed. The aged die, and unfortunately they often die alone because we have defined our lives without them. The poor, the racially discriminated against, and the poorly educated die earlier than do other members of the North American culture. Violence is a daily phenomenon in every city, large and small, of North America, yet we still pretend that life goes on in predictable, orderly ways.

The second limitation of this model is that we often do not adjust our beliefs to fit reality. For example, there is nothing in the nature of things that demands that the older generation outlive the younger. We all know that infants, children, and young adults can and do die, but we often act as though children were born with a guarantee that they will not die until they reach their seventies. The death of a child calls into question our feelings of security and control, including our belief in God as the benevolent guide of the universe.[27]

Death Education of Children

It is clear that the death attitude system most prevalent in North America today does not provide persons with the tools they need at the time of a death. We need to accept the reality that, each time we say "goodbye" to someone, it could very well be the last time—and teach our children the same. All relations are time limited. When we educate children about death, we are only teaching them reality. Death is not just a possibility; it is a certainty for all of us.

As other contributors to this volume have shown, adults often assume that the idea of death is harmful to children or that they are incapable of understanding the limits of life.[28] Neither of these assumptions is accurate. We must not allow our own fears and insecurities to prevent children from facing reality as it truly is. A more positive approach is described here: "I often question whether we're teaching our children what they need most to understand—the profound interdependency of all life; the yin-yang interplay of personal responsibility and freedom; the fact that life is sorrowful and the more we love the more we know pain. I am constantly searching for ways to teach my children the deep solace of kindness in the face of change, loss, and inescapable death."[29]

Once children know about death, their world is irreparably altered. This is one of the most difficult lessons one must learn.[30] Yet it is only in the realization of the limits of our resources that we can get the most from their use. It is only in the realization of the limits of life that we appreciate the fullness of life. The Trappist monks have a saying that one does not have one's feet on the ground until after one has put someone into it. It is wrong to hide this truth from our children. They will learn that truth. It should not be in spite of the adults who care for them.

Conclusion

Herman Feifel tells us that one of humanity's most distinguishing characteristics, in contrast to other species, is its capacity to grasp the concept of a future—an inevitable—death.[31] Fear of death takes many forms and enters into consciousness in many ways: fear of going to hell, loss of identity, loneliness, feelings of rootlessness and having to face the "unknown" with minimal mastery. It is only by confronting the limitations of the North American death attitude system that we will cease to feel confused about death and finally learn how to live.

Notes

1. J. Owens, *A History of Ancient Western Philosophy* (New York: Appleton-Century-Crofts, 1959), 9.
2. R. Descartes, *Meditations on First Philosophy* (1641), trans. L. J. Lafleur (Indianapolis: Liberal Arts, 1960), 32.
3. E. L. Miller, *Questions That Matter* (New York: McGraw-Hill, 1984), 8.
4. H. Smith, *The Religions of Man* (New York: Harper & Row, 1986), 348, 412, 311.
5. A. Eddington, "New Pathways in Science" (1935), quoted in L. M. Regis, *Epistemology* (New York: Macmillan, 1959), 7–8.
6. L. S. Stebbing, "Philosophy and the Physicists" (1937), in *Knowledge and Value*, ed. E. Sprague and P. W. Taylor (New York: Harcourt, Brace & World, 1967), 261.
7. W. L. Reese, *Dictionary of Philosophy and Religion* (Atlantic Highlands, NJ: Humanities, 1980), 577.
8. Saint Thomas Aquinas, *Summa theologica* 1.2, in *Basic Writings of Saint Thomas Aquinas*, ed. A. C. Pegis (New York: Random House, 1945), 22.
9. R. Kastenbaum and R. Aisenberg, *The Psychology of Death* (New York: Springer, 1972), 193.
10. P. Ariès, *The Hour of Our Death* (New York: Knopf, 1981), 47.
11. P. Ramsey, *The Patient as Person* (New Haven, CT: Yale University Press, 1970).
12. N. C. Kowalski, "Anticipating the Death of an Elderly Parent," in *Loss and Anticipatory Grief*, ed. T. A. Rando (Lexington, Mass.: Heath, 1986).
13. C. Goldscheider, "The Social Inequality of Death," in *Death and Dying: Challenge and Change*, ed. R. Fulton, E. Markusen, G. Owen, and J. L. Scheiber (Reading, MA: Addison-Wesley, 1978), 101.
14. V. Navarro, "The Class Gap," *Nation*, 8 April 1991, 436.

15. G. Pappas, S. Queen, W. Hadden, and G. Fisher, "The Increasing Dispar-ity in Mortality between Socioeconomic Groups in the United States, 1960 and 1986," *New England Journal of Medicine* 329, no. 2 (1993): 105.
16. E. Becker, *The Denial of Death* (New York: Free Press, 1973), 4.
17. H. Ozmon and S. Craver, *Philosophical Foundations of Education* (Colum-bus: Bobbs-Merrill, 1990), 248. R. Kramer, "Ed School Follies: The Mis-education of America's Teachers" (1991), in *Taking Sides: Clashing Views on Controversial Education*, ed. J. W. Noll (Guilford, CT: Duskin, 1993), 349.
18. D. Lester, "College Students' Attitudes toward Death as Compared to the 1930s," *Omega* 26, no. 3 (1993): 220.
19. W. James, "Sentiment of Rationality" (1879), in *Essays in Pragmatism by William James*, ed. A. Castell (New York: Hafner, 1959), 13.
20. Becker, *The Denial of Death*, 15.
21. T. Flynn, "Dying as Doing: Philosophical Thoughts on Death and Au-thenticity," in *Thanatology: A Liberal Arts Approach*, ed. M. A. Morgan and J. D. Morgan (London, Ont.: King's College, 1987), 200.
22. T. Rando, "The Increasing Prevalence of Complicated Mourning: The Onslaught Is Just Beginning," *Omega* 26, no. 1 (1993): 47.
23. Ariès, *The Hour of Our Death*, 559.
24. D. Leviton, *Horrendous Death, Health, and Well-Being* (New York: Hemi-sphere, 1991).
25. E. Becker, *Escape from Evil* (New York: Collier Macmillan, 1975), 99, 114.
26. H. Feifel, "The Meaning of Death in American Society," in *Death Educa-tion: Preparation for Living*, ed. B. R. Green and D. P. Irish (Cambridge, Mass.: Schenkman, 1971), 20.
27. K. J. Czillinger, "Advice to Clergy on Counseling Bereaved Parents," in *Parental Loss of a Child*, ed. T. Rando (Champaign, IL: Research, 1986), 468.
28. C. A. Corr, "Reconstructing the Face of Death," in *Dying: Facing the Facts*, ed. H. Wass, R. Neimeyer, and H. Bernardo (Washington, D.C.: Hemisphere), 31.
29. A. Valley-Fox, *Sending the Body Out* (Somerville, MA: Zephyr, 1986), quoted in C. Glendinning, "The Politics of Death," *Utne Reader*, no. 47 (1991): 87.
30. J. D. Van Dexter, "Anticipatory Grief: Strategies for the Classroom," in *Loss and Anticipatory Grief*, 161.
31. H. Feifel, "Psychology and Death: Meaningful Rediscovery," *American Psychologist* 45, no. 4 (1990): 537.

PART THREE

TREATMENTS AND THERAPIES THAT CAN HELP CHILDREN COPE WITH DEATH

Chapter Twelve

Care of the Dying Child

ANN ARMSTRONG-DAILEY

C. Everett Koop, former U.S. surgeon-general and prominent pediatrician, stated that nothing changed the lives of his family more profoundly than the dying and death of his son David. What a sense of powerlessness and vulnerability to learn that a child has a life-threatening illness! How do we care for and support the dying child while at the same time personally trying to tolerate the intolerable?

Ann Armstrong-Dailey is the founding director of Children's Hospice International. She is on the board of directors of St. Mary's Hospital for Children in Bayside, New York, and serves on the advisory boards of Hospice, Buffalo; the Children's National Medical Center; the Women's International Center; and the Cancer Research Foundation of America. She is past recipient of the Washington Woman of the Year Award (1987), the Dame Cicely Saunders Award (1987), and the Living Legacy Award (1989). She is coeditor, with Sarah Zarbock Goltzer, of Hospice Care for Children *(New York: Oxford University Press, 1993).*

Each year in the United States alone approximately 100,000 children die. Moreover, over 7 million worldwide are seriously and chronically ill. A child's serious illness creates unique challenges not only for the child and family but also for the health care professionals providing their care. In this chapter, I show how to turn this difficult situation into a strengthening and bonding one for the family.

Explaining Death to Terminally Ill Children

Although the following guidelines for explaining death to children were written for children with cancer, they can be adapted to any terminal illness:

- Talk with your child in language he or she can understand. Complex medical terms are generally less effective than simple language describing where in the body the cancer is located, what will happen in the treatment, and what the goals of the treatment will be.

- Try to confirm in your own mind that your child understands what you have said. Let your child explain back to you how he or she comprehends what has happened. Then help clarify any areas of confusion or misunderstanding that still exist.

- Explain what caused the cancer or how it started. If the cause is not known, it is important to tell this to your child. Children, particularly younger ones, often believe in "magical" powers, that wishing something "bad" on someone can cause them to be ill. It is important to clarify that cancer is a medical condition and not brought on "magically" by anyone.

- Allow time for your child to express his or her feelings. Many feelings usually accompany a serious illness in a family, and these can and should be shared among family members.

- Encourage a positive approach. Although the effects of some cancer treatments may be potentially upsetting for children, understanding the goals of the treatments and the expectations of improvements helps greatly.

- Reassure children that, despite their illness, they will continue to be cared for and loved.[1]

Care of the Dying Child

Strength in fighting and coping with illness can be greatly enhanced by support and understanding from those you love and who love you. Children need to have the opportunity to be included and contribute to this process, to help strengthen the family's efforts together.

Understanding the Needs of the Child

Timmy was five years old when he died, alone, in a leading children's hospital. Because Timmy's health-care providers and parents alike felt that they had failed when his prognosis became terminal, they withdrew from him emotionally. Sadly, Timmy was left with the impression that his illness was his fault.

With help, Timmy's death could have been less isolating for everyone. Dying children, their parents, and their caregivers all need to know that what they are feeling is normal. Timmy needed to understand that he did not do anything bad to cause his parents to withdraw; his health-care providers needed to know that they could continue to care even when they could not cure; and Timmy's parents needed to understand that they were in no way to blame for Timmy's illness. With appropriate help, they could have all been able to share with Timmy the yellow butterfly he drew just before his death, bearing the words "I Love You Mom." Open communication and understanding between the child's caregivers, the child, and the family is essential.

Children are often aware they may die before their parents, and health-care providers are willing to admit to the possibility. Adults must be willing to listen, and truly hear, what the children are asking and telling us about their illness. They will let us know what they want to talk and know about.

Understanding the Needs of the Family

Families face many difficult challenges in caring for a child with a life-threatening condition. These challenges are not only emotional but financial and logistic as well.

Any long-term health care can be financially draining to a family.

Some financially disadvantaged families may also face the more basic challenges of not being able to get themselves and their child to a doctor (owing to lack of available transportation), to provide proper nutrition, or to stay home with the child (owing to work or other demands).

A child's serious illness and death, and often the financial strain associated with it, can ultimately lead to separation or divorce, substance abuse, or dysfunction within the family as members try to cope. To avoid this, family members need to communicate about the differences in their grieving styles and each other's coping mechanisms.

Understanding the Needs of the Health-Care Provider

Health-care providers are trained to cure. When they cannot cure, they may feel a sense of failure and tend to pull back emotionally from the child for whom they have been caring. These feelings are natural. Health-care providers need help to enable them to care even when they cannot cure and to prevent the effects of burnout and overwhelming grief, especially following multiple deaths. They need time to cope with the loss of a patient and to grieve, to receive acknowledgment of their personal loss by coworkers, to have opportunities to share and discuss their feelings in a caring, empathetic, and understanding environment.

Since professionals in the health field do not enter practice academically, intellectually, or emotionally prepared to deal with death and dying, they must learn to cope with professional anxieties arising from such experiences. This requires an adjustment period for the professional, a time for working through his or her own feelings about death, dying, and life's end.

Professionals can develop ways to cope with anxieties related to catastrophic diseases and terminal illnesses. Social workers and other health-care professionals who are helped to come to grips with their own feelings can then give strength and support to patients and relatives. The patient can be helped to die with dignity and self-respect. Families can be helped to come through a traumatic experience with some semblance of mental health.[2]

How Hospice Programs Can Help

What Is Children's Hospice Care?

Currently, children's hospice services are provided to an estimated twenty-four hundred children in the United States each year (according to a 1992 National Hospice Organization survey, 1 percent of the 240,000 hospice patients are children). Children's hospice care has grown considerably over the past decade—in 1982, about four out of an existing twelve hundred hospice programs were able to treat children. Today, according to a National Hospice Organization survey, virtually all the 1,935 existing hospice programs will consider accepting a child as a patient.

Children's hospice is a concept of care providing physical, psychological, social, and spiritual support to children with life-threatening conditions, their families, and their health-care professionals. It is a team approach bringing together physicians, nurses, social workers, therapists, teachers, clergy, administrators, and volunteers, with the child and family as the leaders of the team.

Children's hospice care is provided in many settings—at home, in a hospital, in a hospice facility, or in some other inpatient setting. It is a comprehensive approach that includes physical care for the child; pain and symptom management; psychosocial support for the child and family; respite care; staff support for health-care providers; special services, such as transportation; and bereavement follow-up with family members. The hospice and/or home-care program, the hospital, or a community-based program coordinates these services, depending on the needs of each individual community. Generally, hospice programs will coordinate the efforts of caregivers already treating a child as well as providing any additional services the child and family may need.

Bernard Nigro (chief of psychiatry, Alexandria Hospital, Alexandria, Va.) regards hospice care as "preventive medicine" for the patient's loved ones since as many as 80 percent of his patients have problems stemming from unresolved grief.[3]

Helping the Child, Family, and Health-Care Provider

The goal of children's hospice care is enhancement of quality of life for the child and family as defined by each child-and-family unit. This type of care allows for a specially designed care regimen that meets each child and family's specific needs. It allows the child the greatest opportunity possible to enjoy each remaining day. The focus of hospice care is life and living—making a positive difference in the life of the seriously ill child as well as in the ongoing lives of their family members and health-care providers.

Children's hospice care allows the parents the opportunity to maintain their role as primary caregivers. It allows the family the chance to participate in the decision-making process surrounding their child's care.

Many children's hospice programs are developing ongoing staff support mechanisms, providing a setting and an opportunity to discuss responses and emotions in dealing with chronically or terminally ill children and patient death. These programs allow the care provider the time necessary to heal, thus enabling them to help the families deal with their loss.

Palliative Pain and Symptom Management

Relieving the ill child's pain and other symptoms, as much as possible, is an essential part of children's hospice care. By allowing a patient in pain some semblance of comfort, we can help them live each day to the fullest. Hospice programs attempt to design pain-management procedures that can be provided at home as well as in the hospital: "The patient must be made a partner in this process, encouraged to evaluate his [or her] needs, communicate them, and share in the determination of how best to manage the symptoms."[4]

Home Care

Home care is a commonly selected alternative for caring for a child with a life-threatening condition. Many children prefer the comfort of home, surrounded by loved ones, to institutional care. Home care also allows the family a feeling of control and enables them to maintain a more "normal" environment with all family members present. Hospice programs can help coordinate home and institutional care with community-based home-care programs.

Respite Care

All families caring for a seriously ill child need a break at one time or another. Such long-term, intense care requirements can be emotionally and physically exhausting to the family, discouraging their ongoing involvement in the child's care.

Hospice support services can provide respite care, giving the family and the patient a healthy sense of independence as well as the opportunity to rest. Respite care can rejuvenate family members, enabling them to continue to provide effective support to each other.

Anticipatory Grief

When a child is diagnosed as terminal, family members begin experiencing grief. It is important for the hospice or hospital care team to identify and help family members cope with this grief as it arises.

The family must understand that it is normal to feel a vast array of emotions and that it does not mean that they are giving up hope. This process is very important in helping them when the child ultimately dies.

Bereavement Care

Hospice programs recognize that, after a seriously ill child dies, the family members will continue to need support. Hence, they provide bereavement services in order to help families cope with the anger, blame, and hopelessness. Each family member will experience the emotions of grief differently and at different times and may need to revisit their grieving process for many years. Siblings will need to "recoup" the loss during each cognitive development stage.

To help grieving parents, the following guidelines for caregivers may be useful:

- Take the initiative to contact the parents.
- Don't judge their grief reactions; instead listen to them.
- Give practical help.

- Repeat information as needed—the stress of the situation may preclude one from grasping it the first time.
- Don't offer platitudes or artificial consolation.[5]

Siblings of the sick child can be profoundly affected by the death of their sibling as well as his or her ongoing illness. The following guidelines can be helpful in addressing some of the unique challenges faced:

- Spend time with children, explaining again and again what happened and answering their questions.
- Share your own memories and feelings with children.
- Use physical touch as a way of reassuring and comforting children.
- Tell children how much the deceased child loved them.
- Reassure children that it is not likely that anyone else (particularly the parents) will also die in the near future.
- Encourage children to express their own feelings and thoughts in their own ways.
- Continue to allow the child to have responsibilities around the house as a way of "normalizing" life.
- Give simple directions or utilize reminder lists for things that need to be done (children, as well as adults, have a hard time remembering while they are grieving).
- Encourage children's involvement with their friends and peers.
- Recognize that there are no magic words. Avoid saying, "I know how you feel."
- Avoid comparisons between the surviving children and the deceased sibling.
- Let children know that feeling sad, angry, or scared is okay for adults and for children and that crying is okay (even for boys).
- Allow laughter and fun times, which do occur even in the midst of great sadness.[6]

Where to Go for More Information

To locate a children's hospice program or specific children's hospice-related services in a particular area, or to obtain more information on children's hospice care and resources available for children, families, and health-care providers, contact:

Children's Hospice International
700 Princess Street, LL
Alexandria, VA 22314
(800) 2-4-CHILD or (703) 684-0330
Fax: (703) 684-0226

For valuable publications and other resources on bereavement and coping, contact:

The Good Grief Program
Judge Baker Children's Center
295 Longwood Avenue
Boston, MA 02115
(617) 232-8390

The Rainbow Connection
477 Hannah Branch Road
Burnsville, NC 28714
(704) 675-5909

For more information on children's hospitals in a particular area, contact:

The National Association of Children's Hospitals and Related
Institutions
401 Wythe Street
Alexandria, VA 22314
(703) 684-1355

For a directory of hospices in the United States, contact:

The National Hospice Organization
1901 North Moore Street
Arlington, VA 22209
(703) 243-5900

Notes

1. Excerpt from "A Family Crisis: Explaining Cancer to Children," by Lois Lorenz, M.S.W., is adapted by permission of the Center for Help in Time

of Loss, River Vale, NJ. Copyright © 1986 by the Center for Help in Time of Loss.

2. Bernice Catherine Harper, *Death: The Coping Mechanism of the Health Professional* (Greenville, NC: Southeastern University Press, 1977), 18.

3. Bernard A. Nigro, personal communication, 1983.

4. Robert A. Milch, *Palliative Pain and Symptom Management in Children and Adolescents* (Alexandria, VA: Children's Hospice International, 1985), 14.

5. Ann Armstrong-Dailey and Sarah Zarbock Goltzer, eds., *Hospice Care for Children* (New York: Oxford University Press, 1993), 129.

6. Ibid., 150.

Chapter Thirteen

"I Thought about Death All the Time . . .": Students, Teachers, and the Understanding of Death

ROBERT G. STEVENSON

There is an increasing awareness in North America of the need for death education in our schools. Sensitive teachers, counselors, and nurses can play a vital role in helping bereaved children and their classmates cope with the death of a loved one. Helping children become aware of their own feelings of anguish and assisting them to express their emotions appropriately are significant coping skills in working through children's grief. The need for preventative education in the area of loss is clear today. The time to begin was yesterday.

Robert G. Stevenson, Ed.D., has taught a death education course to the students of River Dell High School in Oradell, N.J., for over twenty years and is cochair of the Seminar on Death at Columbia University. He is a nationally certified death educator and grief counselor whose work has been widely published on topics related to loss and grief. He is active in both the International Work Group on Death, Dying, and Bereavement and the Association for Death Education and Counseling, where he was honored in 1993 with the Death Educator Award. As editor of What Will We Do? Preparing a School Community to Cope with Crises *(1994), he offers insightful resources and techniques for implementing death education in the classroom and counseling settings.*

Dear Teacher:

My children are returning to school today. They are not the same children that were in your classes last week. Their father, my ex-husband, died, and they are grieving his death. I am asking you, as their teacher, to understand and, if possible, to help them at this difficult time. Please understand that their behavior may change. Their grades may be affected. They have been hurt, and they are sad . . . angry . . . guilty . . . unsure of just what they feel. Their lives have changed and are no longer the way they once were. I hope that we can work together to help them understand and accept what has happened and to move ahead from here.

A Caring Parent

Most teachers will never receive a note such as this. In fact, we seldom receive any sort of information from home about the illness or death of someone important to a child. Unfortunately, without knowledge of such a loss, teachers may respond to the changes in the bereaved child's behavior in ways that only make matters worse. This chapter is directed toward teachers, parents, and other caring adults who want to help children and young adults cope with grief in the classroom.

Good communication between teachers and parents is the first step in helping the children in their care. Parents need to inform all their child's teachers about the death. Teachers must not be reluctant to acknowledge the child's loss and learn from books such as this what they can say or do to help. If the important adults in a child's life fail to react to a death or answer a child's questions about it, it can cause confusion, anger, and even guilt in the children the adults seek to protect.

As we have seen in earlier chapters of this volume, the death of a loved one can produce a variety of emotions in a child: fear, anxiety, anger, guilt, sadness, numbness, and self-questioning. These feelings vary from child to child and even from day to day. Just as there are a variety of feelings that a young person may experience, so are there many ways in which the young person may behave because of those feelings. Young people react to emotional shifts in their lives in a variety of ways, and the same basic feeling can result in very different behavior in different young people.

"I Thought about Death All the Time..."

A young person who is grieving a death may demonstrate some, or all, of the following behaviors in the classroom.

A drop in academic performance. Young people who have experienced the death of a loved one may appear to be daydreaming or to have a short attention span when they are actually dealing with important life issues that may make it hard to concentrate on academics. With elementary school children, this drop in performance is most often seen in language skills (reading and writing). Adolescents may manifest this performance drop in math or science. Even increased effort or more study time may not counter this drop.

Academics are not the only area affected by grief. These young people may also devote less time to or have less energy for sports, friends, or social activities.

Somatic complaints. The school nurse is sometimes the first one to see behavior changes in a bereaved student. An increase in visits to the nurse's office may simply indicate a bereaved child's need for attention or reassurance. However, just because a child is grieving, it cannot be assumed that his or her complaint does not have a physical origin. Grieving children who come to the nurse's office with somatic complaints must first have their physical condition assessed. The school nurse should always begin by assuming that a child's complaint has a physical origin.

In elementary school, if the child says, "I am hurt," ask, "Where on your body have you been hurt?" and, "How have you hurt yourself?" Encourage the child to be as specific as possible. If the child says, "I don't feel well," say, "Be more specific; how exactly don't you feel well?" If possible, avoid leading questions, such as asking about specific ailments. In response to such questions, some children will say yes to everything.

After listening to the child's complaints, take his or her temperature even if the child is not feverish. This helps validate their complaint and can show them that someone is listening and paying attention. If the temperature is elevated, the complaint is probably physical in origin. If the temperature is normal and there are no other indications of physical distress, the child can be allowed some time to lie down, a brief "time out" from the school day. At that point, the nurse can say, "Sometimes, when something is bothering us and we don't know how to talk about it, we may feel it in our bodies. Is there anything that is bothering you?"

High school students are better able to express themselves verbally, but this does not always mean that they will choose to do so. Since they have more support options, including peers, counselors, trained peer listeners, teachers with conference time, or athletic coaches, adolescents are more discriminating in seeking help. Unless they already see the nurse as a helpful, caring person, they will seek other sources for bereavement support. However, students who seek to cope with their grief through denial may manifest their grief through somatic complaints in the same manner as younger children.

Self-injurious behavior. A student who feels guilt connected to a death may seek to be punished in an attempt to cope with that feeling. This self-injury may not be deliberate. Some children suddenly appear to be "accident prone" after a death. These accidents can be a way of dealing with guilt. A pattern of self-injury as a means of coping with grief can also become a factor in risk-taking behavior and, in extreme cases, may even lead to life-threatening behavior. Surviving risky behavior can produce a short-term drop in stress levels, but, unless the real cause is addressed, the stress will return. In the case of repeated accidents or injuries, the school nurse is again a key person in the school's response. A pattern of repeated injuries, even minor ones, should be communicated to parents and guidance personnel.

Punishment seeking may also occur in the form of behavior that causes disciplinary action to be taken against the student. Lateness getting to school, cutting class, arguing with teachers, vandalism, or other types of acting out may be a way for the bereaved student to deal with guilt. In these cases, it is the school disciplinarian who will be best able to see patterns in such behavior. He or she is in a position to know if such behavior by a student is a change from the past. Such acting out can be part of a grief reaction. Such a reaction may explain behavior without excusing it. It is important for the vice-principal or other administrator to know when counseling may be needed more than punishment. All appropriate school personnel—classroom teachers, the school nurse, coaches, club advisers, and administrators—must be included in a schoolwide communication network to ensure appropriate responses to a bereaved student.

Fighting. When a loved one has died, it never seems "fair." If no one is found to blame, a bereaved youngster may need an outlet for unresolved anger, or this strong emotion can lead to fighting and other aggressive behavior. Typically, this type of fighting is not confined to a single episode. Younger children exhibit a pattern of fighting, sometimes with little or no provocation. This fighting is a change in the child's behavior. Older adolescents may not fight as frequently, but their fights are more intense and can be most violent. This attempt by bereaved students to use fighting as a release of anger can be overlooked in today's schools, where violent outbursts are becoming more frequent.

In these cases, punishment has little effect. In fact, it can cause more anger and, in the long run, more fighting. A better method of stopping such fighting is to provide students with an alternate method of physically releasing anger. Young children and adolescents alike can participate in physical exercise such as bowling or archery as an effective substitute for fighting. Contact sports, where force is directed against another person, have not been as helpful in breaking a pattern of fighting.

No change in behavior. Some young people postpone reaction to a death. In trying to avoid the emotional pain that accompanies grief, they deny the loss and may postpone grief for years. Holding in grief in this way may take even more energy than the grief itself.

Educating Children about Death

Our schools are charged with the education of the whole child. Events that block learning have to be addressed. Death and the grief that follows are just such events. Therefore, parents, teachers, and school counselors must help children come to terms with their grief.

Some administrators and teachers act as if death is an issue that affects only a handful of students in our schools. But, even in the lives of the most protected children, death will often intrude. Death can claim grandparents, parents (one child in twenty will have a parent die before the child's senior year in high school), siblings, peers, or neighbors. The death of a classmate, teacher, or administrator can affect every child in a school. Even the death of an animal can affect a child.

Moreover, one in 750 students dies each year, chiefly from accidents that can be both violent and unexpected. Violence is not always accidental, and ours is an increasingly violent society. The homicide or suicide of a young person can affect all those young people who learn of the death. When four teens took their own lives in a small New Jersey town a few years ago, the media coverage of the event touched the lives of many thousands of young people nationwide. Many young people fear a violent death, and, as an old adage says, the fear of a thing may be even worse than the thing itself.

Deaths portrayed in the media can have a similar effect. A newspaper columnist wrote of the effect of an antigun political commercial on her four-year-old daughter. The television spot was designed to draw support for legislation to ban semiautomatic weapons. After seeing a watermelon blown apart at the end of the spot, the young girl asked, "Do those guns kill children?" and began to cry. That child now fears being shot and suffering a bloody, violent death. She is about to start school, and she will bring her fear with her to the classroom.

The school, then, has a particular role to play in helping young people understand death. The term *death education* refers to the formal instruction that deals with dying, death, loss, or grief and their effect on individuals, families, and schools.

Before setting up a program, parents, teachers, and administrators must agree on answers to the following questions: When should death education take place? Who should teach it? What should be taught? How should it be taught?

When should death education take place? A child's age is an important factor in answering this question. However, it is not age alone but also the developmental level and experience of the child that should determine the content and methodology of death education. It must be understood that there is no one age when death education is generally right for children. For this reason, no single curriculum is suitable for all students. With the wide difference in developmental levels that exists in most elementary school classrooms, these students need specific lessons that address specific needs. As students grow, they are able to understand more abstract concepts, and these can then be incorporated into the curriculum.

Who should teach it? Educators who wish to implement death education programs in schools must first have addressed the death-related issues in their own lives. They must then learn the effects of grief and the special ways in which young people react to a death. This knowledge is not automatic. A comprehensive approach to death education requires formal preparation and ongoing staff development for the teachers, counselors, and administrators involved.

The preparation of death educators and counselors is too important to be left to chance. The Association for Death Education and Counseling has developed a certification program for death educators and grief counselors. The presence of certified staff members can ease parents' concerns. Certified staff members can also offer in-service courses to other staff members to ensure a schoolwide response in times of crisis or when a death affects the entire school community. An ongoing program of staff development can ease the fears of educators. Staff members are more likely to act to assist bereaved students when they believe that they can do something that will help and not hurt the child.

What should be taught? Younger children's needs are simple. There are three basic concepts that young children need to understand as soon as they are able. First, they need to understand that *death is universal*; all living things will eventually die. Death does not single out bad people for punishment, nor do only the good die young. Second, they must learn that *death is permanent and irreversible*. Some students will believe that a soul, or atman, or spirit, or life force, is immortal and will continue, but wishing, praying, or good behavior will not bring back a deceased loved one. Finally, *dead people can no longer feel anything*. A dead person cannot be hot, cold, or in pain. These lessons are not learned in one sitting and may have to be repeated again and again as children grow or as they encounter new deaths. These concepts provide a foundation for future knowledge and experience.

The first question that children want answered is, "Why?" Why do people die? That question, asked by so many young students, is still being asked by some adolescents and even adults years later. Some years ago, the wife of a colleague died. My son had not known the woman well, but to help him understand what had happened I read him a book by Sara Bonnett Stein, *About Dying*. The story concerns the death of a pet bird, the death of a grandfather, and the different ways in which three siblings of different ages try to understand and cope with these deaths. After hearing the story, my son, Robert, looked up at me and asked, "Why do people die?" I explained that people die because they are so sick (not with a cold, but *very, very* sick), so badly hurt, or so very old that their bodies won't work any more. Many people, including doctors and nurses, may try to help, but the person's sickness or hurt can't be fixed (a term even young children come to know in connection with their broken toys). When the body stops working, the person dies. This is the same explanation that I have used with young children in schools after the death of a student, parent, or teacher.

Robert sat for a moment thinking; then he asked, "Are you old?" He could see that I was not sick or hurt. Behind his question was another one that concerns children. If you die, what will happen to me? I tried to answer both questions. I told him that I was older than he was and older than my students but that his mommy and I would do all that we could to stay with him and love him for as long as we could. Even if something happened to us, we had made sure, with a piece of paper called a will, that someone would always be there (grandparents, an uncle and aunt, or some other person he knew loved him) to care for him. He paused again and asked, "Is Nana old?" Nana, his great-grandmother, was at that time in her mid-eighties. "Yes," I answered, "Nana is old." He asked if we could see her that weekend, and I agreed.

This preschool child had encountered the death of someone he knew, asked people he trusted questions about what happened, and used logic to find a way to cope with this new understanding and even to do things with loved ones before another death took place. All our talks had taken place in an atmosphere of mutual trust and open communication. Each of us tried his best to understand what had happened, and we worked together toward a common goal—a better understanding of death and the grief process. Educators must try to ensure that the same atmosphere is present in any attempt at addressing the topic of death in schools.

How should death education be taught? As in the case described above, a story makes an excellent starting point to open a lesson about death or grief. This is the most common method of introducing death education with young students, and it has even been used effectively in high schools and colleges. *There's No Such Thing as a Dragon* by Jack Kent is such a story. In it, a young boy wakes up one day to find a dragon in his room. When he tries to tell his mother about it, she says that there is no such thing as a dragon. Each time she says this, the dragon grows in size. Finally, the boy says that the dragon *does* exist, and it shrinks to its former size. After hearing this story, young children have described the dragons in their lives. They can see how talking about a problem, such as a death, can make it seem a bit smaller. Older students see that the dragon's size can be controlled by others. They can then be asked about the "dragons" in their lives. How big are those dragons, and why is that the size they want them to be?

Since its effects can seem therapeutic, some people refer to this use of a story or book as *bibliotherapy*. A student can identify with a character in the story. The experiences of that character can assure a student that new thoughts or feelings are "normal" because others have had them too. Some fiction provides a catharsis of pent-up thoughts and feelings by allowing the student a safe outlet for laughter or tears. The logic and problem solving of children can be developed and given a positive direction through stories.

High school adolescents can be more skillful than younger children at hiding their feelings. Their questions may be not just unanswered but never asked. Their greater ability to understand abstract concepts makes death education different with adolescents, but it is not necessarily easier. Every answer offered to them may only raise more questions. Topics addressed in high school death education courses include such broad topics as death, dying, grief, and loss. More specific lessons address topics such as support systems (such as family or friends), institutions (such as hospice), suicide prevention, HIV/AIDS, funerals, mourning rituals, cross-cultural studies of death rituals and coping, death-related themes in music and art, or moral dilemmas (such as assisted suicide, euthanasia, capital punishment, or abortion). Classes vary between school systems and instructors. Lectures and reading assignments in death education are similar to those in other subjects, but follow-up testing and interviews with students and their teachers show that students retain more information and show greater transfer of this knowledge to other subjects. Their test results also show higher levels of academic performance than these students demonstrate in other English, history, or science courses. Traditional academic skills such as public speaking, research, and writing are an integral part of most secondary death education courses. Death education students in one high school have spoken at professional seminars and training programs, published articles in professional journals, and helped create student and faculty support groups in other schools.

There is something about the topic of death that transcends age and formal academic preparation. One high school senior attended a graduate medical symposium in New York City on the topic of complicated grief. This young man was a special education student with several learning disabilities. After sitting with a medical doctor at lunch and discussing the last presentation, the doctor asked this teenager, "Are you a medical student, or are you an undergraduate?" The topic of death is so important to many of these young students that past educational labels are set aside and their performance can surprise even themselves.

The needs of students of every age challenge educators to identify those needs and to find ways in which to help students acquire knowledge and skills to meet those needs. Adolescents report feeling more control over their lives after a death education course. They state that they can often communicate more easily with family members and that they can more easily identify sources of support to help them deal with critical issues in their lives. They also say that, for many of them, looking at death has given life greater meaning.

Crisis Response Plans

A death can occur at any time. Therefore, the time to plan a response is *not* in the emotional aftermath of such an event. The ideal time to create plans that will be used during and after a crisis is before such a crisis occurs. Crisis response plans cannot take away the sadness that follows a death. However, if such a plan is in place and is implemented by people (educators, community leaders, parents, and students) prepared to play their roles, it may be able to keep the pain from being worse than it has to be. Such a plan can address rumors. It can answer questions. It can help students and staff express their grief. Death education programs and crisis response plans must be developed in our schools if they are to be in place to help students when the need arises. However, such programs should not be developed by educators alone.

Death education and crisis response plans should start with a task force of educators, parents, and community leaders. In the case of adolescents, students may be included as well. This task force can then identify possible needs of the students and district should crises occur. It can identify school and community resources available to meet such crises. Protocols can be developed for use should a crisis occur. Key personnel can be identified for training, and programs for staff development can be started. Lines of communication among all concerned parties can be opened and maintained. Finally, other schools or districts can be brought into systems of mutual support so that no school or district need stand alone in time of crisis.

Death education has not been without its critics. The Eagle Forum is a conservative political lobby led by activist Phyllis Schlafly. This small but vocal group claims that death education undermines family values and parents' authority. It has distributed information that seeks to portray teachers and parents as adversaries. Such an adversarial relationship would involve all parties in a destructive confrontation whose real victims would be the children for whom both groups care.

The Parent's Role in Death Education

Parents are the first and most important educators of their children. When the schools begin to help with this task, the lessons taught by parents must be understood and, whenever possible, supported and reinforced. It is parents who decide whether there will be a spiritual dimension to a child's understanding of death. They begin to shape the child's understanding of death, by addressing or by avoiding the topic, long before the child steps into a classroom, and that process continues throughout the school years. When no attempt is made to understand and support the work of parents, a teacher can be perceived as an adversary. This can greatly complicate the tasks of teachers and parents alike. Death educators need to understand the role of parents in the process of education. These educators must be willing to work cooperatively with those parents in the best interests of the students. Any school program that seeks to help students cope with death-related concerns must be based on ongoing two-way communication between teachers and parents. When parents and teachers are adversaries, limited energy and resources are wasted in fighting between groups that should be natural allies.

Critics who attack, block, or end programs without offering positive suggestions can be divisive and hurt the very people they claim to care about. However, teachers and parents are all too human and, even with the best of intentions, do make mistakes. For just this reason, critics can be helpful by pointing out errors and shortcomings so that they may be corrected or improved. Such criticism can allow programs and teachers to help the children they serve more effectively. A caring parent is one person who can play that role.

Parents should play an active role in preparing their children to face the problems that they will encounter when death intrudes on their world. Parents can play such a role in working with educators to ensure that death-related school programs benefit their children. In working with educators, parents should consider the following steps:

Ask questions. As students are often told, the only bad question is the one that is not asked. If a parent has concerns, the same concerns may well be shared by others. Educators have an obligation to parents to explain the *why* behind courses and policies.

Communicate with the school. Channels of communication can be difficult to establish in times of crisis if they have not been there previously. Attend parent-teacher nights; speak to teachers, counselors, and administrators so that you have met the people your child sees each day. If you have concerns, contact the school.

Begin death education programs where none exist. Death education can start with one concerned person. This person can be a teacher, counselor, administrator, or parent. The program can be started as a separate course or as part of an existing curriculum. There are prepared course outlines and curriculum materials available (such as *Growing through Grief* by Donna O'Toole or *Dimensions of Loss and Death Education* by Patricia Zalaznik), or the teachers and school system may wish to write their own.

Know the curriculum and the teacher. Death-related courses can be intellectually and emotionally powerful. To best help their children, parents should be aware of the content of their child's courses and meet the teachers involved. Firsthand knowledge of what a child is learning in school is also a powerful antidote to baseless rumor.

Know what school policies exist and when they will be implemented. All members of the school community should be active in establishing crisis-response policies. Parents' action (or inaction) should be based on certain knowledge of what is being done in school, not on second-hand information.

Point out when new policies may be needed. It is not only educators who can identify policies that may be needed in our schools. Parents should not be reluctant to use the lines of communication that they have opened to suggest policies or programs that they would like to see available to their children in schools.

Conclusion

Children cannot be isolated from the topic of death. But educators and parents can form a powerful alliance to inform and support children as they face this difficult topic. For example, River Dell High School, in Oradell, New Jersey, has had a death education course for over twenty years. Parents and students have played an active role in establishing policies and in developing and evaluating the curriculum. Children from over two thousand families have taken this elective course, and the parents and the community have been overwhelmingly positive in support of the course and the policies that have developed out of it. The reason why may well have been summed up by one student. At the end of the course, she was heard to say, "Before I took this course, I could never talk about death, but I thought about death all the time. Now that I've had this class, I talk about death all the time, so I don't have to worry about it anymore." Death education allows all of us—students, teachers, parents—to "talk about it" with each other. Perhaps in this way we can make death a little less fearful and understand the roles that it will play in each of our lives.

References

Kent, Jack. 1975. *There's No Such Thing as a Dragon.* New York: Golden Books.

O'Toole, Donna. 1989. *Growing through Grief.* Burnsville, NC: Mountain Rainbow.

Stein, Sara Bonnett. 1974. *About Dying.* New York: Walker.

Stevenson, Robert. 1994. *What Will We Do? Preparing a School Community to Cope with Crises.* New York: Baywood.

Zalaznik, Patricia. 1992. *Dimensions of Loss and Death Education.* 3d ed. Minneapolis: Edu-Pac.

Chapter Fourteen

Special Needs of Bereaved Children: Effective Tools for Helping

MARYANNE SCHREDER

Support groups are dynamic, effective tools for meeting the special needs of bereaved children. In a safe place, grieving children share their pain and their successes, telling and retelling their personal collage of stories. As they form new friendships— crying and laughing together—they gradually accept their losses and rebuild their lives.

Mary Anne Schreder, a pioneer in the field of loss, death, and grief, is an accomplished, highly regarded counselor, teacher, and speaker and a recipient of "The Caring Institute" award. Schreder personally realized the need for emotional support through her experience of multiple losses. She created the Centre for Living with Dying in Santa Clara, Calif., to support anyone with a life-threatening illness or the trauma of having a loved one die. The Centre has grown to become the most comprehensive bereavement agency in the United States and has served more than 700,000 people in the past twenty years, including hundreds of bereaved children.

My First Teacher: Experience

My Own Grief as a Child

I never planned to go into the "death and dying" business, nor could I anticipate the events that would change the course of my life.

Living in the freedom and beauty of the Pacific Northwest, for many years it was easy to perpetuate the denial of death that I had learned as a small child. But, when I was in the third grade, I witnessed the death of a classmate. He was sitting next to me on the school bus. I said goodbye to him when he got off the bus and waved. As he crossed the street, he was struck and killed by a car, and the last I saw of my friend Danny was his yellow rainslicker lying on the ground. That was my first experience with death. After the church service, our class never spoke of him again, nor was his name ever mentioned.

My grandmother died very suddenly when I was eleven years old. After traveling by car over two thousand miles and with no preparation whatsoever, I walked into Grandma's house to find her in the open casket in the corner surrounded by carnations, her favorite flower. My brother and I were whisked away to the safety of a bedroom with aunts and uncles, while my mother knelt and cried. I remember lying in bed all night, the bed she had died on, listening to the rest of the family at the wake. I remember the next day, when I was alone, kneeling at the casket, saying a prayer, telling Grandma how much I already missed her. I reached over to touch her hand, and I was shocked to find how cold and hard it was. And I remember my heart filling with fear. I remember telling my brother about the hand. My uncle overheard and said you are not supposed to touch the dead. It seemed like a long time before I had my mother back from her grief, but we rarely talked about Grandma, and no one talked to me about my grief. For years, I couldn't stand the smell of carnations.

When I was a married woman of twenty, with a career goal of interior design, death marched into my life with a vengeance. My best friend and neighbor, Norma, died of kidney disease. As young married mothers, we shared all that a friendship can be. In a six-month period of time, her illness was diagnosed, it progressed, and her life ended. Norma died in July, and the grief I experienced following her death, the intense sadness and loneliness, was but a quick preparation for what was to begin in less than seven months.

I was twenty-one years old and the mother of two young children. The dawn was literally just breaking on Mother's Day when my life was shattered by the suicide of my husband with a high-powered rifle in the living room of our home. Within six months, after moving back to my home town, I discovered I was pregnant, witnessed my father experiencing two heart attacks, and delivered a baby who died at birth. During the next ten years, death came again and again into my life; I lost eleven family members and close friends. My father died. I remarried and gave birth to my third child, and my second husband died of heart disease. Having been widowed at twenty-one and twenty-eight, I tried to pick up the broken pieces of my life. I was isolated and alone with my overwhelming grief; the help I needed did not exist.

Shortly after the suicide, I sought solace from a parish priest. I desperately needed to talk about the horror I had witnessed. His words to me were that I needed to pray and to trust in God. I tried to talk to my obstetrician; he gave me painkillers and tranquilizers for comfort. I sought the help of a psychiatrist. After listening to my whole story and asking me only three questions, he suggested that I needed to get a hobby. I paid money I didn't have for this advice, and I left his office feeling more isolated than before.

While trying to help myself survive, to find meaning in all the madness, I found myself working in the "helping" professions. For several years, I worked in alcohol and drug treatment programs and with runaway teens and rape victims. For six years, I worked with suicidal individuals and facilitated groups for those who had actually attempted the act. It was during that time that my mother-in-law, my very dear friend, died of cancer. During the course of her illness, we had the opportunity to share her dying and to complete our relationship lovingly. Her courage in openly facing her death with me and my children led me to start the Centre for Living with Dying.

In 1975, with the help of close friends, mental health and medical professionals, and clergy, I began to establish the Centre for Living with Dying. Located in a 130-year-old mansion in Santa Clara, California, the Centre offers a caring, nonjudgmental presence to all facing a life-threatening illness, dying, or the grief of having a loved one die. Through a variety of nonresidential crisis intervention services, individual and group counseling, and education and training programs, the Centre has served more than 700,000 people in its first nineteen years of existence. Staff and over two hundred extensively trained volunteers provide a broad spectrum of services for all ages and issues. Clients come from all age groups (three to ninety-six), from all religious, ethnic, economic, and professional backgrounds.

Despite the success of the Centre and my commitment to this work, my greatest challenge was yet to come. After an intensive weekend training for volunteers, I received a telephone call that my nineteen-year-old son had been critically burned in a freak fireplace explosion. He was severely burned; his arms were amputated, and he lost all his facial structure. Together we lived in the burn unit for twenty days until he died. Scott died on the fifth of December; his funeral was on the ninth, my birthday on the eighteenth; then holidays and the New Year came. My life was shattered again, more than it had ever been. I had to question whether I could continue as the executive director of the Centre for Living with Dying. Scott's courage in his dying and depth of pain and the need for help of the hundreds of people coming through the Centre doors renewed my commitment, gave me the hope and strength to continue.

What the Denial of Death in Our Society Has Created for Our Children

One of the Centre's programs is designed specifically for children and young people. I wanted them to have a place where their grief would not be trivialized, minimized, or negated. Young people are so often harmed by the well-meaning intentions of adults. Some people want to protect children from the reality of death. Some don't know what to say or do to make things better. Others are lost in their own grief and cannot or do not know how to acknowledge a child's grief. Adults often deny, camouflage, or sugarcoat the reality of the pain. We don't tell the truth; we are not or cannot be emotionally present; we fail to recognize and to validate our children's feelings. These actions and responses rob our children of the ability to express their grief and to heal their shattered lives. The following examples demonstrate the common threads of avoidance, fear, and denial perpetuated by our society and inflicted on our children. Recognizing these threads and our own past experiences is the key to exploring more positive and effective ways to support our young people.

Avoiding the Issue

Robbie came to the Centre when he was three. His mother died of cancer when he was two years old. Her dying and death were never truthfully discussed, so he made up his own explanation. The only picture he had of his mother showed her standing in the backyard beside what he called an "oka" bush. He remembered her sneezing when she stood by it. He concluded that his mother died from sneezing, and he was subsequently afraid of and upset by the bush and sneezing.

When Katie was seven years old, her mother died of a brain tumor. During her mother's illness, Katie always brushed her mommy's long hair. Her mother's hair often fell out in large gobs on the brush. No one ever explained to Katie the reason for or effects of chemotherapy. After the death, the children were placed in foster care. Some weeks after the funeral, Katie became visibly upset and cried at the sight of her own hair in the hairbrush after her foster mother had washed her hair. Katie was convinced that she, too, had cancer. After all, when your hair comes out on the brush, you die.

When she was eleven, Nancy's favorite aunt died suddenly. She was not allowed to go to the funeral and was shielded from all discussion about the death, services, and burial. She could also sense that no one wanted to talk, even to mention the aunt's name. It was as though the aunt had never existed. As this was her first encounter with death, Nancy was left to the confines of her vivid imagination with no information whatsoever from relatives who wished to protect her. Three years later, Nancy came to the Centre after a good friend and classmate was killed in an automobile accident. She had withdrawn totally and refused to talk. She wanted desperately to accompany her classmates to the funeral, but the fears and frightening images of a funeral that she had generated when her aunt had died prevented her from attending.

Little Ears Overhearing

Alicia was six years old when her father died of AIDS. He became progressively weaker as his health deteriorated, but no one told Alicia why. Several weeks after the funeral, Alicia became hysterical one morning, refusing again to eat the breakfast her mother had prepared for her. She ran sobbing to her room and refused to talk. On her second visit with the Centre counselor, she talked of her fear of eating breakfast prepared by her mommy. When asked what the breakfast consisted of, she spoke of the bacon and sausage but began to cry when she talked about the eggs. After all, her mommy always cooked eggs and bacon for daddy, and Auntie Alice had told someone on the phone that her daddy had died of "eggs."

Brian was five and was expecting a new baby brother soon. His mother delivered the baby, but the infant lived only two days. The parents were so grief stricken that Brian had not been told of the tragedy. He was brought to the hospital to visit and to comfort his mother. Before he was told the truth, he overheard an aunt tell someone that his mother had lost his baby brother. He remembered that, when he had lost his bicycle, his aunt had bought him a new one. Brian, therefore, asked his aunt when she would surely get him a new brother. The aunt realized the family needed grief support to tell Brian the truth about the death of his baby brother.

Euphemisms and Their Effects

Every day, on the way to day care, when four-year-old Rebecca and her mother drove past the church, Rebecca became frightened and began to cry. She was unable to verbalize her fear. In a session with a counselor, it was discovered that her father's funeral had been held in that church. Having not attended the funeral or graveside services, Rebecca believed what she had been told: her father was still "asleep" in that church. She was angry at God for keeping her daddy there and for not letting him wake up and come home.

Christopher was four years old when his father died suddenly of heart disease. He told the Centre counselor that he had gone to heaven with friends and relatives in a big car to visit his father. Heaven was filled with beautiful flowers. His father was in a box all dressed up in a blue suit. What really impressed him the most about heaven was drinking from the "really neat" water fountain. He kept talking about wanting to go back to heaven.

Kevin's grandfather was killed in a hunting accident. Seven-year-old Kevin was taken to his grandfather's funeral, but, in his parents' deep sorrow, very little was explained to him about what to expect. The casket was closed. The church was filled to capacity. In the eulogy and at the reception following the funeral, he heard so many mourners express that the community, family, and friends had lost such a great man. Three months later, Kevin accidentally dropped and broke his grandfather's coffee mug. He became enraged and shouted, "I am going to Wyoming to find my Grandpa. He is not lost, and I will buy him a new mug."

Lying to Protect the Family Image

A twelve-year-old boy, Carlos, was told that his father died in an automobile accident in the mountains. One month later, while helping his uncle clean out the garage, Carlos opened his father's tool box. Neatly taped to the inside lid was a typed letter addressed to Carlos from his father, explaining why he had committed suicide. Carlos was devastated because he had held the belief that God had called his father to heaven via the car accident. In boldfaced type, he learned the truth—that his father chose to end his life and to leave his son behind.

Suzanne's older brother died of cancer, or so she had been told. One of her friends approached her one day at high school and asked her how long her brother had had AIDS. She was devastated. She went home to confront her mother, who refused to talk about it. Suzanne took down every picture of her brother in the house and pretended she had never had a brother.

After a heated argument, Michael and Nicole, fifteen and twelve, witnessed their father shooting and severely wounding their mother before turning the gun on himself. When asked by friends at school what had happened, they explained that their father had been cleaning his gun. Adults aren't the only ones who protect the family image when some deaths occur.

Misinterpretation of Physical, Behavioral, and Emotional Problems

Shawn had been an A student in high school, a star on the football and track teams, and a student body officer. His father had been a popular swim coach at the same school when he died suddenly of a heart attack. Within nine weeks following his father's death, Shawn's grades had dropped significantly. He was making continuous excuses to the coaches as to why he couldn't work out and practice. What Shawn was not telling anyone was that each day he was experiencing heart palpitations that were becoming more severe. He was convinced that he, too, was going to die of his father's disease. He was unable to share his feelings and fears with his bereaved mother or with any of his friends. Shawn did not realize that physical symptoms are a normal reaction to grief.

David adored his second-grade teacher, who had died unexpectedly. When the class pictures were distributed, he became visibly upset and disruptive. He voiced anger that Mrs. Brown, his former teacher, was not in the class photograph. Other staff criticized his reaction as totally inappropriate, not realizing that this was his way of expressing deep sorrow and loss.

Lani was twelve years old when she experienced recurring nightmares about suffocation. She was so upset that she stayed up as late as she could watching television, refusing to go to sleep. She insisted that a light be kept on in the hall and that her bedroom door be kept open, requests she had given up at the age of three. After counseling, she revealed that, for years, she was afraid her mother had awakened in her casket and then had suffocated for lack of air.

Mathew's father committed suicide by hanging. Mathew and his younger brother discovered the body in the garage when they came home for lunch. Three months after his father's death, thirteen-year-old Mathew exhibited signs of severe depression and suicidal behavior, unrecognized by his family until they came for counseling. Mathew withdrew into his room; his schoolwork suffered; he began giving his prized possessions to his best friends. He told the counselor that he wanted to join his father. He said that he had heard on a television program about suicide that children of suicidal parents are often at risk.

He coupled this information with what he was learning in a science unit on genetics. He concluded that he had inherited his father's "suicide gene."

Steve drove three of his buddies to the beach for the day. On the return trip, after a couple of beers, Steve lost control of the car on a dangerous curve; the car careened off the highway and hit a tree. Steve was slightly injured. Two of his three friends died, and the other was in a coma. The seventeen-year-old boy experienced tremendous guilt, despite reassurances from the police that he had not been legally intoxicated. Even support from his own family and his friends failed to alleviate his overwhelming feelings of remorse, guilt, and responsibility. His relationships with others were laced with angry outbursts and withdrawn indifference. According to his family, this once careful driver now refused to use his seat belt and drove recklessly as though challenging death himself.

Providing Effective Support

The case histories presented above are not the exception but the rule. The feelings and reactions of the young people are not unusual but very typical of what we see at the Centre for Living with Dying every day. These cases all illustrate problems children have in dealing with death after the fact. However, these same issues often begin with the onset of serious illnesses or impending death, and all the support skills and activities discussed below can be initiated before as well as after a death.

In the past few years, society has progressed in its attitudes about discussing sex and providing sex education. We have learned from experience that failure to discuss the topic doesn't make the problems of unprotected sex and teenage pregnancy disappear. Avoidance merely causes the issue to go underground, often to surface in destructive ways. As with sex education, the best possible way to deal with death is with honesty, to provide as much age-appropriate, accurate information as is needed at any point in time. Children are very straightforward and direct: what they ask for is what they need to know—no more, no less.

Concrete and specific support skills create a positive and pro-active atmosphere to help children living with the issues of loss, death, and illness recover and heal. These tools are effective whether responding to a crisis or providing ongoing support to an individual, family, or group. From our experience, these approaches and activities work but must be used with sensitivity, understanding, and awareness of how powerfully we as adults affect and influence young people.

Create a Safe Environment

Children need a sense of safety and peace in order to risk sharing their feelings. We must validate the depth of their crisis and pain. We need to let young people know that we cannot make things better or "fix it." We are there to provide support—to walk with them and to help them on the road toward healing.

Don't rush or push. When children first come to the Centre, we give them a thirty-minute tour. We do the talking—explaining our program, and showing pictures of other children, but giving no counseling at all. We want to make the children as well as the adults, teachers, and parents feel totally at ease. What follows are some opening activities that we find useful.

Stuffed animals. In dealing with younger children individually, we have them choose their own stuffed animal to be their friend for the day from a menagerie of "sad," "scared," "mad," "lonely," and "happy" animals. If the children feel comfortable, we ask them to explain their choices.

Drawing. We draw pictures together. The children are asked to illustrate their feelings, their family, or whatever is on their mind. They may draw cartoon characters or monsters, which are safe avenues of expression. For example, one five-year-old boy drew pictures of Superman getting killed in a variety of ways—he was shot, stabbed, and beaten. They boy's father had been murdered, although the details had been withheld from him. His Superman drawings were a safe way to express his awareness of his father's brutal death. At the same time, the counselor draws, too, along the same theme and gives the child the opportunity to ask questions about that drawing—and older children and teenagers often ask very specific and probing questions.

Puppets and dolls. Puppets and dolls are excellent ways to create a nonthreatening avenue for dialogue. Even quiet, nonverbal children may feel safe enough to respond through the puppets or dolls they have chosen. This same technique is an effective way to deal with issues of physical, sexual, and emotional abuse.

Clay. Clay provides an artistic and physical outlet for young people's emotions. Music playing in the background is a calming distraction. Having children create with their eyes closed sometimes allows more freedom of expression. This method unleashed the feelings of a six-year-old girl who had seen her mother collapse and die of an aneurysm. She subconsciously molded her mother's body lying on the floor, which she had sat beside for hours.

Music. Particularly appealing to teenagers, music can be an excellent avenue for communication. Sometimes we ask young people to bring us their favorite music. Listening carefully to music we often avoid, we can then ask what it is about the song that makes it a favorite—what is touching or moving—and about what music reminds them. The music becomes a conduit through which to discuss issues and feelings. Many children like to create their own songs, whether nursery rhymes or rap music, all of which are mirrors of their pain and struggle as well as of their love and hope.

Just being there. In a group session, participants are encouraged in the beginning to share what brought them there. Did they come to the group by choice or by force (family pressure, referral from school, as a condition of probation, etc.). The question itself is an icebreaker, usually leading to laughter and joking. After this initial question, participants can just sit and listen, sharing their own experiences and feelings only when they are ready to do so. The option to "pass" is always available and creates the safe, nonthreatening environment.

Acknowledge and Validate Feelings

"You'll get better; time heals." "You're too young to understand." "I know how you feel." "Just don't talk about it, and it will be all right." "It's not right for you to feel that way." "Don't cry; you need to be brave for the others." These are the phrases that young people often hear from well-meaning adults. What they really hear is avoidance, condescension, and minimizing of their pain. In order to help them, we need to aid young people to identify and express their feelings and then to validate the magnitude of their grief. Recognize as normal these feelings of anger, guilt, sadness, fear, physical distress, and even relief, whether these feelings are expressed verbally or nonverbally. Then listen and explore the details, giving the child the opportunity to communicate the specifics from the inside out.

What Young People Say

Many of these comments were taken from two videos developed by the Centre for Living with Dying. One focused on adolescent grief, the other on younger children's responses to a sudden death. In both videos, actual clients from support groups at the Centre shared candid comments in unscripted scenes:

- "I didn't expect people to die in a hospital. They go there to get better."
- "I don't want to hear 'I'm sorry' or 'I know how you are feeling' or 'Don't cry, everything will be okay.' They don't know how I am feeling."
- "I never saw so many adults cry. They won't talk to me. I don't know what to do."
- "I feel bad. Why didn't I cry?"
- "I don't understand; it's not fair. Other people have mommies that are alive."
- "I'd rather hear 'I'm sorry' than nothing at all."
- When I walk down the hallways at school, people avoid me. They don't know what to say, so they don't say anything at all."
- "I want someone to say, 'I'll listen if you want to talk. I don't know what to say to you, but I care about you.'"
- "The pain and hurt don't go away. They get easier to deal with."
- "It's been three months, and no one even mentions my brother. Everyone expects me to get on with it, but it still hurts."
- "I need to know I am not alone."
- "People care; they just don't know how to show it."

- "I wanted a choice about going to the funeral."
- "I used to be the son. Now I have to be part father. They all told me I am the man of the house now."

Facilitate Healing through Age-Appropriate Activities

Children and adolescents react to the same situations differently depending on their age and their relationship with the deceased. For example, after their father died, the five-year-old clung to his mother for long periods and the fifteen-year-old brother acted out his anger by screaming and storming out of the house. The key to effective communication is to interact with children according to their developmental age and to their relative comprehension of death. We need to meet them in their own landscape of understanding—neither talking down to them nor talking above their heads. Don't superimpose an adult perspective on a child's question. When in doubt, ask specifically what it is that the child really wants to know. For example, a six-year-old boy, Ray, wanted to know about his brother's fatal car crash. The parents hesitated and balked, assuming he wanted to know all the details of the incident. A counselor later discovered that all Ray had wanted to find out was whether his brother had a bloody nose or broken finger, just as Ray had had during a recent baseball game. The activities suggested offer options to engage young people in dialogue, to help them express feelings that may have been deeply buried or repressed. It is not a matter of right or wrong, only selecting the vehicles to promote discussions of feelings, fears, and thoughts.

Activities for Young Children

Special memories. Give the child the opportunity to talk about positive memories and special times shared with the person who is dying or has died. These memories will include humorous, happy, and heartwarming experiences as well as traumatic and painful recollections.

Memento sharing. Encourage young people to share or to talk about specific objects associated with their loved ones. At the Centre, clients have brought in clothing, jewelry, photographs, and even plants that connect them to and allow them to speak about those who have died.

Portraits. Ask the young person to draw a picture of his or her loved one who has died and to talk about it. Some children draw pictures of heaven, of cemeteries with flowers, or of funeral services. Others instead draw the person happy, well, and whole, enjoying a favorite activity.

Read books. There are many excellent books about death or dying written for various age groups. Read them together, and discuss the child's reaction to the book.

Worry rocks. Let children choose or find a special rock that can be decorated or left plain. That rock can be placed in their pocket and held when needed. It becomes their special stone, absorbing some of the pain and giving back courage and strength.

Puppets. Have children select or construct their own puppets, and encourage puppet shows and dialogues. Puppets provide a form of "psychodrama" for kids.

Colors. Many times, when children have trouble expressing their feelings, help them identify a color that describes how they are feeling. Ask them about the color—what does that color mean, feel like, or represent.

Snack time. As a reward, incentive, or break, snack time is important. Children must continue to eat despite their grief, and favorite foods can be a comfort or simply another way to reach a child.

Activities for Adolescents

All the activities listed above are appropriate and effective with adolescents and even adults. In grief, we need to access and to heal the little child within. In addition, the following techniques are also applicable to older children:

Journal. Ask young people to keep journals, recording specifics about what they miss about a person, the ebb and flow of their feelings, how their day went, and what hurts the most. Many people find it easier to write down their feelings than to express them verbally. A possible next step is to have them read the journal out loud.

Letter writing. This is taking care of unfinished business. Ask the individual to write a letter directly to the person who is dying or has died, including what they wanted to say but for some reason never did. Letters can be written as well to living family members, hospitals, God, even to oneself.

Anonymous questions. In a group setting, give participants the safety and opportunity to write down questions anonymously, which the whole group will then address. No question is dumb or stupid. Knowing others struggle with the same issues lessens the sense of isolation.

Role playing. Another effective therapeutic tool is role playing. Participants in groups set the scene, providing their own problems and experiences for the group to act out. Young people can choose which role they want to play—themselves or another player in their scene.

Collages. Have young people construct collages to express their life today without the loved one, the treasure chest of memories in their hearts, or their journey of grief. Feelings are released and acknowledged through the symbols selected, and the collage may provide a total visual picture of the grief experience.

Self-portrait in grief. Sad, mad, glad, scared—any of these emotions may be reflected in the drawings. Often healing can be clearly seen in how the self-portraits change over time.

Say Good-bye: Ceremonies of Closure

There are very easy yet positive ways actively to say good-bye to a loved one, and these simple ceremonies are particularly successful with young people. These activities afford the opportunity for closure and celebration of love and life:

- Plant a tree.
- Plant a potted flower to keep.
- Light a candle next to a photograph.
- Draw a picture or create a card for a special occasion or for placement in the casket or grave.
- Release a helium balloon with a message attached for the person who died.
- Make a "prayer feather" (a decorated feather to which special thoughts or wishes are attached), and release it to the wind.

- Sing a song or write a poem to perform on the anniversary of the death.
- Create a plaque or mural in honor of a loved one.

Build a Matrix of Support for the Ongoing Journey of Grief

It is critical to recognize that grief is a long journey for people of all ages. Many companies give adults a three-day bereavement leave, which is scant acknowledgment of the intricate process of grief. In many states, we give children a one-day bereavement leave from school. We expect people to "get their grief over with"—or at least to stop talking about it—in a brief, unrealistic, prescribed period of time and to return to business as usual, functioning fully. People, particularly young people, need more time, support, acknowledgment, and permission to grieve.

Anniversaries, holidays, birthdays, date of the death, and special events can all act to bring the grief to the surface. For example, calls to the Centre for support increase dramatically before the winter holidays, Mother's Day, and Father's Day. Many powerful feelings related to a death may be delayed or drawn out or may resurface months or years after a death. Jerry, a fifteen-year-old high school sophomore, was generally a good student. His grades fell rapidly as the anniversary of his father's suicide approached. Be aware of such potential problem times in order to prepare for them. Acknowledge that holidays or special occasions may stir up feelings and memories. As they approach, include children in planning of activities to include a celebration of the memory of the person who died. Continue family traditions, incorporating some of the activities previously mentioned, or create new ceremonies that bring meaning and healing to the anniversary.

The Centre's philosophy is to work with people in grief for as long as the need exists. The needs of bereaved people ebb and flow, sometimes requiring different approaches, activities, or types of support. It is imperative to work with all components of a child's life. This can be accomplished by developing a matrix of support methods: working with the family in counseling, offering peer support groups at school or a counseling center, and providing individual support.

Trauma, pain, and loss can teach us how not to take life and those we love for granted. Suffering can show us the importance of living each moment to the fullest. We can survive personal tragedies and emerge strengthened by them. One of our young people said it so eloquently after the death of her mother: "I have walked the road of grief. I can now look back at how far I have come. I can look to the future with the new tools for living that grief has given me. I have learned how to celebrate life and love."

Chapter Fifteen

Using Story, Film, and Drama to Help Children Cope with Death

SANDRA L. BERTMAN

We can teach children a great deal about death through the metaphor of visual arts—story, film, and drama. Stirring situations evoke in them a rich source of insight, catharsis, and self-discovery. "Arts cannot stay the flight of the birds of sorrow, but they can help children to better appreciate and endure them."

Sandra L. Bertman, Ph.D., directs the Program in Medical Humanities at the University of Massachusetts Medical Center, Worcester. A humanist, teacher, and clinician with thirty years of experience, Bertman is internationally respected for her work on death and grief. Dealing with people of all ages, her multimedia slide presentations are tailored to meet the needs of her audiences. This widely published author has received many honors for her work in the field, including the 1991 Outstanding Death Educator Award from the Association of Death Educators and Counselors. Her book Facing Death: Images, Insights, and Interventions *(1991) is a unique, helpful handbook for educators, health-care professionals, and counselors.*

Death is all around us. In recent years, our children have been as-saulted daily with images of death that have become increasingly vio-lent and troubling. Although the world has changed substantively over the past generation and our children have become less "innocent," the fundamental questions a child asks about death, dying, grief, and loss remain the same: Why did somebody or something die? Why do I feel so sad? What happens after death? Am I going to die too? The adult's responses, regardless of the sophistication of the child, must remain simple, honest, consistent, and loving.

While real-life situations are full of the immediacy of the moment, they do not generally provide the best introduction to death for a child. In fact, the real-life scenarios that are commonplace fodder these days for our newspapers and television shows are often full of frightening images and may serve only to create misconceptions and an excess of fear around the subject. One way to approach death that works well both for children who have experienced the loss of a loved one and for those who have not is through books and other visual media. Experi-encing death through fiction or film allows us to observe others under-going this challenge from a safe distance. Hearing characters express thoughts and anxieties about death that we ourselves share can be reas-suring and helps objectify the necessity of coming to grips with this aspect of the human condition. When we experience the uncomfort-able feelings of a protagonist, we come to realize that not all life's mys-teries can be solved any more than death and grief can be avoided.

The following discussion focuses on the various materials, from books to filmstrips to video to films, that serve for children as a good introduction to the subject of death and dying. The materials are geared mainly to preschool- and elementary school–aged children, al-though I have included some suggestions for older school-age children and adolescents. While teachers may find these resources most useful, parents, therapists, and other caretakers, especially facilitators of small groups, may also find them helpful.

Several good books and films approach the subject of death by por-traying the loss of a pet. Parents and teachers may wish to begin here for several reasons. First, it is a loss that a child is very likely to experi-ence, given the generally short lifespan of common pet animals. Second, and more important, even though children may develop very close attachments with pets, the loss of a pet is rarely, if ever, loaded with the psychological and emotional issues of dependency and survival that are evoked, say, with the death of a parent or sibling. With preschool or young school-age children, the teacher might begin with the filmstrip *My Turtle Died Today*,[1] in which a sick turtle dies despite the efforts of the boy's father, teacher, and the pet store owner. Billy, the protagonist, and his friends question one another about the realities of death. Together they bury the turtle and then find a litter of kittens to which to transfer their attention. My only reservation about this piece is the almost immediate replacement of the turtle with the kittens. Lacking is the necessary lapse of time before replacement can be tolerated and not viewed as betrayal or inability to care. In this otherwise charming filmstrip, the creators might have spent some time exploring feelings of sadness and longing and might even have addressed the issues of guilt and anger.

I'll Always Love You is a lovely story that provides such a critical interim.[2] Young Elfie's sadness at the death of his aged dog is tempered by the remembrance of having told it every night, "I'll always love you." The parents who had continually scolded the dog when she got into mischief and the siblings who loved the dog but never told her so experience a more difficult grief reaction. Offered a new puppy by a neighbor, Elfie refuses, giving the dog's basket instead to the puppies with the explanation, "Someday I'll have another dog, or a kitten, or a goldfish. But whatever it is, I'll tell it every night: I'll always love you."

The Dead Bird extends the theme of remembrance even further through children who continue to visit the gravesite of the bird they have buried: "And every day, until they forgot, they went and sang to their little dead bird and put fresh flowers on his grave," writes author Margaret Wise Brown.[3] An important point to stress is that, after the funeral, one does not necessarily forget. Indeed, one can remember both with joy and with tears. One can "miss" a pet or another human and feel wistful or sad but not grief stricken. Memories of the loved one last a long time and may be recalled deliberately or unexpectedly. Unfortunately, although the phrase "until they forgot" gives the children of *The Dead Bird* permission to move on, it suggests that forgetting is the expected goal. It does not acknowledge the importance (and consolation) of memory.

The Yearling, a book classic and feature-length film that deals directly but sensitively with life-death issues on many levels, is an excellent bridge to beginning discussions about the death of humans.[4] While the book is probably most appropriate for children twelve years and older, the film version can be useful for children as young as eight or nine years. Amid the rhythmic cycles of nature—the birthing of animals, the changing of the seasons—the young protagonist, Jody, is faced with many of life's harsh realities, including not only the death of animals but also of Fodderwing, his young disabled friend.

In one touching scene, Jody and Fodderwing discuss what heaven must be like. Later, when Fodderwing dies, Jody and his siblings "cry their eyes out." With Jody, they attend Fodderwing's funeral and try to understand his bereaved mother's belief that death represents freedom, an end to Fodderwing's physical suffering. Her vision of a reborn Fodderwing without his handicap, somewhere taking care of the animals he loved, is even more poignant in light of the earlier conversation about heaven between the two boys. By naming the yearling Flag, the name Fodderwing suggested, Jody creates a living memorial not only to the lad and his love of animals but also to the friendship the boys shared.

The Yearling also shows how death can affect all members of the family. Jody's father learns that too much protection can be crippling: a child, however young, must experience his share of disappointment, sadness, and loss in order to grow. Jody's mother, whose method of warding off the impact of losses is to develop a tough exterior, learns to acknowledge her feelings. Ultimately, she too is able to show her son the love she has been withholding, the love she feels.

By living through extraordinarily difficult circumstances such as seeing his best friend die, killing an animal to save his father's life, giving up a beloved pet yearling, and running away as a solution to a problem, Jody slowly becomes initiated into adulthood. Rawlings writes, "He did not believe he should ever again love anything, man or woman or his own child as he had loved the yearling. He would be lonely all his life. But a man took it for his share and went on."[5] This suggests the painful, albeit necessary, transition from the innocence of youth to the often harsh reality of adulthood.

Although Jody is of a different era and lifestyle from today's typical classroom of more sophisticated urban and suburban youngsters, the basic emotions have not substantively changed, and nowhere else is the panoply of death more sensitively portrayed than in the context of Rawlings's naturalistic milieu. In my experience, contemporary readers and audiences learn very quickly to transfer their own experience of suffering and empathize readily with Jody. By the end of the book and film, Jody is no longer a yearling, and, by extension, neither are the young reader-viewers.

Drama and role-play are other ways to encourage children to examine their feelings and test their ideas against those of fictional characters and their classmates. Role-play also provides an opportunity for children to work through their hidden concerns, beliefs, and fears. Very young children enjoy dramatic play and adapt very quickly to make-believe. In fact, they may seem frequently unable to distinguish the real from their fantasy world. Older children may require more guidance in the form of specific scenes or situations.

Dramatic play as a way to express one's feelings is demonstrated in two scenes from *In My Memory*, a classroom television video that portrays a young girl's response to the death of her grandmother.[6] The teacher or discussion leader might want to consider stopping the tape after the opening (expository) scene to give the audience an opportunity to discuss it or even assign characters' roles and initiate a dramatic play to work out the resolution to the story. It is always interesting to watch the audience's reaction to what happens in the video when compared with their own interpretation.

In the first scene, Linda's play with dolls allows her to vent her feelings of guilt ("I didn't always do what grandmother said") and her interpretation that grandmother's death is her punishment ("Grandma left me alone; she didn't want to be with me anymore"). In the second scene, Linda and her cousins are playing "Bang, Bang You're Dead."

The youngsters in the class talk about playing dead to see what it's like (they all have) or confess sheepishly to such acts as having pulled the wings off an insect just to see what death is all about.[7]

Although a bit maudlin and sentimental for some adult tastes, *In My Memory* remains an effective classroom tool. Third- and fourth-grade youngsters identify with Linda's confusion and with her sad feelings of guilt. In fact, the students often call out the questions the protagonist wants to ask her parents *before* she asks them. They understand the parents' inability to talk to Linda, their fear of "breaking down" in front of her. They are also quick to dispel the parents' hollow rationalizations. When a younger cousin asks the whereabouts of Grandma and is told to go play with an older cousin, the class is usually critical. They reason that an adult should talk to the little cousin, explain what has happened, and answer his questions. In follow-up discussions or role-play, the children will often assume this responsibility.

The class accompanies Linda to the funeral and identifies the point at which she understands the meaning of her grandmother's death. When Linda's mother finds her crying in bed that night, mother and daughter talk about the continuity of life ("I was her little girl. You're my little girl. Someday you'll have a little girl of your own") and affirm the value of tears ("It's all right to cry—especially together"). Most third and fourth graders are not comfortable with the ending, which has the mother tucking Linda into bed and shutting off the light. They argue that the mother should not leave Linda alone at this time.

Students often express a desire for an additional scene to the film: Linda three months later. They want to see whether Linda's sadness is still deep ("Will she always feel this way?") or whether she has managed to feel happy or healed. The parents' breaking down is viewed the same way. Youngsters understand that visible expressions of grief demonstrate deep caring, but they need to see that such grief does not last forever. Here is yet another opportunity for the teacher or facilitator to create a role-play situation.

The Day Grandfather Died, a short film also appropriate for classroom use, has a protagonist who does not articulate his feelings as well as Linda.[8] Unlike her, David shows anger. When he learns of his grandfather's death, he rushes from the room, yelling, "No! I don't want him dead!" Students usually have much to say about the way David's parents try to draw him out of his sullenness and isolation ("You're not the only one. . . . You lost a grandfather and friend; I lost my father"). The last scene of the film shows David a few months after the death, reveling in a pleasant memory of his grandfather. When his friend asks, "What's wrong?" David smiles to himself, choosing to keep his thoughts private. He continues to play with his friend without explanation or discussion. Such a scene might well have served as a fitting epilogue to *In My Memory*.

Comparing and contrasting Linda's and David's experiences can be a valuable exercise in appreciating the different behaviors and coping styles that arise in essentially the same situation. Linda can talk to her friends and parents and ask questions ("What's a heart attack?" "What happens when you die?" "Will you die?"); David cannot ("What's bothering you, David?" "Aw, nothing"). Two different religious beliefs are also presented and could certainly be explored through discussion or role-play.

Both Linda and David try to visualize their grandparent's moment of death, and both attend the respective funerals. In the classroom, before viewing these materials, discussion of funerals is often punctuated by nervous laughter. In general, grade schoolers feel it is preferable not to attend funerals. However, after viewing the tape and film and learning about what to expect at a funeral, the idea becomes less frightening. The nervous laughter usually disappears, and the youngsters often conclude that they ought to be given a choice about whether to participate in these rites.

Neither the videotape nor the film offers a perfect model for initiating discussion of these sensitive and deeply personal matters. Perhaps their value lies mainly in what they do not handle well and the way that mishandled situations reflect reality. Death *is not* a natural and comfortable topic for discussion; people *are* concerned about breaking down. In any situation that is so emotionally charged, even the most well-intentioned person can become a blunderer.

The teacher or group facilitator may wish to conclude a unit on death with a series of role-playing exercises that summarize the key issues surrounding grief and loss. Some scenarios that may be appropriate for late elementary or junior high schoolers include the following:

- A babysitter must deal with a six-year-old's dead dog who was just run over in front of the house.
- An older brother tells his younger sibling of their grandfather's death.
- After a dreadful argument with her grandparents, a twelve-year-old girl learns that her grandmother has been hospitalized with a heart attack.
- A young boy visits his dying grandfather in the hospital.
- Two girls pay a condolence call to a friend whose father was killed.
- An eleven-year-old girl is asked what her mother's job is by her classmates, who don't know that she has no mother.

Will Death Education Unleash a Flood of Heavy Emotions?

Yes, of course. But fear of outbursts must not prevent this important process from taking place. Death education is like sex education: nobody wants to be responsible for it, yet everyone recognizes the necessity of having it done well.

After my class one day, a third-grade girl could not stop crying. We talked at length about her exclusion from the rest of her family during the period surrounding her grandfather's death and funeral. Later, her mother explained to me that, in her effort to spare her child the sadness of the event, she forbid any signs of mourning in their home. The girl also missed her grandmother, who was not allowed to visit their house until she, too, could refrain from mentioning Grandpa and prevent her eyes from filling up with tears.

Why, you may ask, did I expose the girl's tortured feelings if nothing "positive" could come out of it? After all, a teacher cannot control or undo a home situation; no teacher can control what happens to her students outside the classroom. But I believe we have no alternative. To avoid discussing such potentially volatile issues is itself a kind of conspiracy to keep troubling feelings submerged. By allowing children to share their feelings and sadness about death, we reduce their anxiety and self-consciousness; more important, we demonstrate to these children that they are not singularly abnormal or peculiar.

After we talked, I asked this youngster whether she felt better. When she answered, "No," still with tears in her eyes, I realized that simply opening a discussion could not be the end of her need to grieve. The girl needed to talk to her parents as well. Unburdening herself to her mother or father would be the second step in her grieving process. The classroom teacher should inform the parents and the guidance counselor of this experience and offer to provide therapeutic ideas and resources. In cases such as these, a number of books that parents and children might read together can be recommended.[9]

I am often surprised by how close to the surface these emotions and concerns lie. The third graders did not want to stop talking—in detail—about their own experiences of loss. Just because they read their parents' signals correctly ("I can't talk to Mommy about Papa's death because he was her father"; "I know not to mention Uncle Harry to Daddy because he was his brother") does not mean that the youngsters aren't ready to explore their anxieties and concerns about death. Given the license to do so, they approach the task with great energy. Somehow, in the free and clear light of the classroom, the demons of the mind lose their potency. The opportunity to express their feelings openly in a supportive and nonjudgmental atmosphere, however temporary, can be tremendously regenerative.

My anxiety at the tears of a sweet ninth-grade girl during and after one of our sessions was relieved by her gratefulness for them. She was consoled by the realization that she could still be moved and proud of her ability to continue to "hurt" for her father, who had died almost three years previously. She recognized her own tears as "tears of love" and was adamant that she would always love her father. It was an important lesson for us as well as a comfort for this girl to realize that her father, taken from her in death, could never be taken from her again. She could and would hold him safe and close, forever, in her heart and memory.

Shouldn't the Teacher Leave Discussions about Death to Parents, Religious Leaders, or Psychologists?

Twenty years ago, one of the most frustrating situations for nurses in my seminars was the doctor's "order" not to discuss the diagnosis with the patient. What a dilemma it was for the nurse who watched patients struggle to make sense of what was happening to them. It is the nurse who is at the bedside continually, even in the wee hours when the patient cannot sleep and wishes to talk. Today we realize that this practice was misguided. No caretaker should be required to detach herself or himself on the dotted line that separates the person from the professional.[10] Professionalism cannot ever mean learning how *not* to respond to human suffering and anguish.

Similarly, the teacher is present in the classroom when a student's pet dies; when a grandmother, teacher, parent, or sibling becomes ill; when a divorce occurs; when a president is assassinated; when a space shuttle explodes during a televised launch; when the home of a child with AIDS is torched; or when a class member is living with a serious illness. She cannot avoid the issue. If she detaches herself from the situation, she will only create a void for her students when they are confused and most in need of help. The teacher *is* the professional. She must also be able to assess the needs of all the students, be aware of her own limitations, and above all have the appropriate resources available when referral is necessary.

Can Teachers Help Educate Parents about Children's Responses to Death?

Knowledge is power for parents who may feel inadequately prepared to assume the responsibility of educating their children on the subject of death and loss or who may be uncomfortable dealing with emotionally laden situations. It might make sense to offer such parents one or two workshop sessions to review the resources and materials used in classrooms. We have often held such "Helping Children Cope" workshops through the school's parent-teacher organization. Having the school counselors and, in some cases, the school nurse available to facilitate discussion on the emotional and practical aspects of these issues might also be helpful.

In one such workshop, a parent felt that we were exaggerating the child's ability to grieve. He related anecdotes that raised the question of the "callousness" of children. In the informal seminar setting, we viewed parallel anecdotes of aloofness in film, television, and classroom materials. For example, in Paramount's *All the Way Home*, the film version of James Agee's *A Death in the Family*, Mary, who is trying to prepare her five-year-old son Rufus for the death of his grandfather, is interrupted and asked, "Do I have to wear my hat?" After being told by Mister Rogers of an assassination, Owl asks whether they can have a picnic. In the aforementioned *In My Memory*, the children are playing "Bang, Bang You're Dead!" at the very moment the relatives are soberly reminiscing about the grandmother just before her funeral.[11]

For adults such scenarios legitimately suggest callousness and a "short sadness span." Yet this is not true; adults must recognize that children can absorb only a little sadness at a time. They mourn differently from adults, and therefore such indifferent-seeming behavior is neither inappropriate nor indicative of a lack of concern. Children have a way of grieving as they are able. They can manage to dose themselves appropriately.

Some adults are horrified by the explicit visual images of death that appear in these classroom materials, such as the grandmother struggling for breath in *In My Memory* or the grandfather clutching his chest in *The Day Grandfather Died*. "Why didn't the filmmaker cut these shots? How gross and sadistic," one parent exclaimed. But children need to see such images because they *are* curious to know whether blood gushes out at the moment of death or whether death hurts. Only by the inclusion of such scenes do we affirm the child's right to know about such ("gross") details and allow them to see that they do not wonder alone.

Parents often raise the same objections about funeral scenes: "How horrible for a child to see the casket lowered into the ground!" "Children should not be present at wakes." Yet, after seeing such scenes sensitively dramatized, most parents acknowledge the value of helping prepare the child for the funeral ritual. They even recognize that seeing the casket lowered into the ground helps convince the child that the dead grandparent is permanently gone.

In one joint session with parents and youngsters, the adults were surprised to hear an eleven-year-old girl talk about her wish to say goodbye and express her love to her dying grandparent. She responded to *The Day Grandfather Died* with, "It's too bad his grandfather died so suddenly; the boy didn't have a chance to tell him how much he loved him." Pursuing this point, I asked the children how they would feel about visiting a dying grandparent in the hospital. There was no squeamishness or hesitation. Yes, the youngsters agreed, they certainly wanted to say goodbye. Yes, they should be allowed into hospitals. Another child wanted to know why the picture that Linda (of *In My Memory*) had made for her grandmother could not be placed in the casket. Thinking she did not understand what death meant and that she believed the grandmother was alive even after burial, I questioned her further. She understood very well that the grandmother was dead, but she added, "Linda had made this drawing for her grandmother. . . . Maybe they'd both feel better. Certainly Linda would." Why not, indeed?

In this joint session, the children confronted the issues with a healthy directness, while the adults remained uncomfortable. Once again, the children helped the adults view this challenging material with new eyes. It was role modeling in reverse. In this case, the children possessed all the common sense, self-assurance, and warmth of what humanness is all about.

What Materials Might Be Suitable for Older Children?

Although appropriate materials are created and available for specific age groups, as already illustrated, they can frequently be adapted for older groups. Nursery rhymes and fairy tales are fun even for the most sophisticated students (e.g., John Ciardi's esoteric analysis of Humpty Dumpty and Lewis Carroll's "Jabberwocky"[12]) and can help drive home the important points.

In the junior high milieu, the most provocative segments that I have taught have dealt with children and adolescents facing their own deaths. The protagonists of *Death Be Not Proud*, *Johnny*, *Admission to the Feast*, *Shira*, *David has AIDS*, and *At Risk* all know their diagnoses, and we become aware, as they do, of their growing ability to confront their deteriorating conditions with courage and dignity.[13]

You See, I've Already Had a Life is a poignant film in which a thirteen-year-old boy with leukemia comes to terms with his life-threatening illness.[14] In the very real home and hospital settings, Paul interacts with classmates, family, and doctors. He talks out his thoughts about not wanting to be treated differently because he is ill and about feeling depressed, even suicidal. As if Paul were a member of their class, one group shared Paul's distresses along with their own. They talked openly about their discomfort with disabled classmates. They wished that the film had detailed the reactions of Paul's schoolmates and close friends. They also wanted to explore the moments of emotional breakdown in the family and test them against those of *All the Way Home* and against their own experiences. Despite the thematic seriousness of the film, they laughed at Paul's substituting cider for a urine specimen. Paul helps viewers bear the unbearable and reminds us of the healing power of humor. He shows us what makes human beings human and how they can be more so.

At the beginning of our unit on death awareness, the students expressed a preference for a quick, sudden death that would happen without warning. Yet they were able to acquire tolerance and respect for Paul. Simply stated, the students learned to grasp a new belief in themselves and in their own potential. Consequently, the class became more willing to entertain the concept of living with a life-threatening illness.

What Materials Are Available for High School Students?

There is no lack of resource material on death for secondary school students. In 1973, a *Time* magazine education section featured an article on "Thanatology 1" and photographed Minneapolis high school students trying out coffins and making detailed plans for their own funerals.[15] The article further reported that some seventy colleges and schools throughout the country had begun offering organized courses on death. Any current newspaper is bound to carry a local story of a class visiting a graveyard, and on any church or synagogue bulletin board one can find advertisements for discussion of such issues as death with dignity, physician-assisted suicide, abortion, and AIDS. In the last five years, the demand for courses or counseling programs dealing with death, suicide, and AIDS has become overwhelming for most high schools, preparatory schools, and colleges. The very real threats of violent death, suicide, and AIDS are much more perplexing topics for the teacher or counselor to address.

High school students have never led insular existences, but the 1990s have thrust them into the maelstrom of violence and death. Even for students who live in relatively safe communities, rap music and heavy metal epitomize the teenager's preoccupation with these themes and offer bleak outlooks with respect to intimacy, ethnic relations, and survival. The fast-paced, high-stakes thrills of contemporary action films, with their renegade, machine-gun-toting heroes, offer violence and megadeath as the new alternative to justice. Many teens continue to follow cult and hard rock performers with names like Suicidal Tendencies, the Grateful Dead, and Metallica. The earlier, more helpless teen fear of annihilation by global nuclear holocaust has been replaced by the more immediate risk of violent death in one's own backyard.

Again, the traditional materials that have been mentioned above can be adapted for the high school audience. The creative facilitator must work, however, to develop the most up-to-date materials for comparison and contrast. Today's top-ten hit is tomorrow's oldie; consequently, in order to hold the typical teenager's interest, any selection of music, video, or film must never seem dated. One way to assure freshness is to solicit appropriate suggestions from the students themselves.

Does Death Education Need to Be a Separate Classroom Unit?

No. Classroom teachers in touch with the day-to-day events in their students' lives can draw connections at appropriate moments. Death need not be the only event that calls attention to loss, loneliness, and manifestations of grief. Entering and leaving adolescence, concluding a relationship, becoming a member of a blended family, and moving to a different neighborhood or school all require change and adaptation to new life patterns.

For any age group, a unit on aging can be useful. How old is old? What's aging all about? Study the lifestyles of the old. William Butler Yeats's "Wild Old Wicked Man" is not the waning gentleman of Anne Sexton's "Old." The loneliness of Brel's "Old Folks," who have lived too long, or the nameless man in the film *Machina* is different from the solitude of the old French woman in *The String Bean* or the gold miner in *Nahanni*.[16] What is the new cloning movement all about if not a re-birthing and coming of age? The old people's chorus "I'd Rather Be Dead than Wet My Bed," the Beatles' "When I'm Sixty-Four," and Yeats's "Why Should Not Old Men Be Mad?" give clear voice to the fears, concerns, and joys of the "golden" generation.

Indian Summer and *Geronimo Jones* are sensitive and insightful treatments of young boys' excitement with change juxtaposed against the termination by progress of old men's roots and lives. Close such a unit with *Adventures of an ∗*, a lighthearted animated film illustrating the repetitive generation gap of the father-son-father cycle ("down they forgot as up they grew," as the poet e. e. cummings might describe it). Children's literature is a marvelous entrée for exploring the bonds between the alpha and the omega generations. Shel Silverstein's parable *The Giving Tree* continues to seem very fresh in classroom discussions today, and Robert Munsch's *Love You Forever*, first published in 1986, is in its thirty-first printing. Required reading for young and old should be *Things I Like about Grandma*, a story about grandmothers raising their own grandchildren, and *Wilfrid Gordon McDonald Partridge*, the tale of a small boy who lives next door to a nursing home. Both books are beautifully and sensitively illustrated.[17]

Social studies, history, and English courses continually include units on war: "Dulce et decorum est pro patria mori."[18] People don't always die *of* something; sometimes they die *for* something. Listen to World War I poetry, to Brooke's "The Soldier," McCrae's "In Flander's

Field," or the World War II air force theme song, "Wild Blue Yonder."
Then contrast them with Sassoon's "Base Details," or e. e. cummings's
"next to of course god america i," or Country Joe and the Fish's "Viet-
nam Rag." Look at war heroism as portrayed in the visual and cine-
matic arts. Contrast Manet's painting *The Shooting of the Emperor Maxi-
milian* (1867) with Dix's *Dying Soldier* (1924). Heroes die for causes
other than country. The love-honor paradox uttered in Lovelace's "To
Lucasta" ("I could not love thee dear so much / Loved I not honor
more") is the theme of Stanley Kramer's film *High Noon*.[19] Big Bad
John sacrifices his life in a mine disaster, and it certainly was more than
country that inspired *Jesus Christ, Superstar* (1973).

A unit on ecology also raises death issues. In Rodgers and Hammer-
stein's musical *Oklahoma* (1943), we are told: "The daisies in the dell
will give off a different smell because poor Jud is underneath the
ground." The repercussions of tampering with the balance of nature
are charmingly treated in a short French film, *Les Escargots*. Follow the
showing with the animated *Life Cycle*, and then take a look at any of
the well-known materials that decry modern medical therapies that
prolong life and dehumanize death.[20] Discussion could revolve around
the living will or the ethical morass of resource allocation.

Oblique or direct, in the classroom or at home, discussions between
teachers and students, parents and children, on matters of life and death
seek to provide both the license and the impetus to confront painful
realities together. I hope that the materials and methods outlined here
will help restore hope to the bleak horizon of our contemporary society, which is so often today darkened by violence and fear. Literary and
visual resources are provocative allies. They provide both outlets for
self-expression and avenues toward self-knowledge, human connection, and what Pascal calls "spiritual insight."

Notes

1. *My Turtle Died Today* (8 min.; New York: BFA Educational Media, 1968).
2. H. Wilhelm, *I'll Always Love You* (New York: Crown, 1985).
3. M. W. Brown, *The Dead Bird* (Reading, MA: Addison-Wesley, 1965).
4. M. Rawlings, *The Yearling* (New York: Macmillan, 1938). One film ver-

sion of *The Yearling*, directed by Clarence Brown (1985), is available from MGM / UA Home Video, Loews Inc.

5. Ibid., 405.

6. *In My Memory* (13 min.; Bloomington, IN: National Instructional Television Center, 1972; distributed by B.S.A. Educational Media, Santa Monica, CA).

7. The question of whether such behavior is "inhumane" and whether inhumanity is innate to the human species might be appropriate topics to address in such a unit. William Golding's *Lord of the Flies* (New York: Coward-McCann, 1954) takes an extremely pessimistic view of childhood savagery. "In the Day of the Robin," a short story by Tony Cennamo (Boston: Equinox Institute, 1971), two nine-year-olds kill a lame bird and then react to the incident. In *Wargames* (19 min.; Boston: Equinox Institute, 1983), one character narrates an innocent tug of war that results in the killing of a goat by a group of young boys on a beach in Tokyo. In another film, *The Magician* (13 min.; New York: Sterling Educational Films, 1982), the question of conditioning or brainwashing is raised as a group of youngsters is introduced to shooting games by a magician in military garb.

8. *The Day Grandfather Died* (12 min., 1970; National Instructional Television Center, Inside Out Series, Program of Medical Humanities, University of Massachusetts Medical Center, Projects in Loss and Grief, 159 Ward St. Studio, Newton, MA 01655).

9. A recommended reading list might include Barbara Pomerantz, *Bubby, Me, and Memories* (New York: Union of American Hebrew Congregations, 1983); Max Lundgren, *Matt's Grandfather* (New York: Putnam, 1972); Bettina Egger, *Marianne's Grandmother* (New York: Dutton, 1986); Audrey Harris, *Why Did He Die?* (Minneapolis, MN: Lerner, 1965); Tia Otilia, *My Aunt Otilia's Spirits* (San Francisco: Children's Book Press, 1987); Miska Miles, *Annie and the Old One* (Boston: Little Brown, 1971); Jennifer Bartoli, *Nonna* (New York: Haravey, 1975); Earl Grollman, *Talking about Death* (Boston: Beacon, 1976); Norman Simon, *The Saddest Time* (Niles, IL: Whitman, 1986); Gwem Everett, *Li'l Sis and Uncle Willie* (New York: Rizzoli, 1991); Sandy Lanton, *Daddy's Chair* (Rockville, MD: Kar-Ben Copies, 1991); Sherry Kohlenberg, *Sammy's Mommy Has Cancer* (New York: Magination, 1993); Arnold Dobrin, *Scat* (New York: Four Winds, 1971); and Lucille Clifton, *Everet Anderson's Goodbye* (New York: Holt, 1983).

10. "Go on, tear yourself off on the dotted line that separates the woman from the social worker" (B. Clark, *Whose Life Is It Anyway?* [London: Grenada Television, 1970]).
11. *All the Way Home* (103 min.; Wilamette, Ill.: Films, Inc., 1963). James Agee, *A Death in the Family* (New York: Avon, 1938). "Mr. Rogers' Neighborhood" is produced by NET Television.
12. J. Ciardi, *How Does a Poem Mean?* (Boston: Houghton Mifflin, 1959), 683–85.
13. J. Gunther, *Death Be Not Proud* (New York: Harper & Bros., 1949); O. Sanderlin, *Johnny* (New York: Pyramid, 1970); G. Beckman, *Admission to the Feast* (New York: Doubleday, 1988); S. Grollman, *Shira: A Legacy of Courage* (New York: Doubleday, 1988); D. Sanford, *David Has AIDS* (Morton Grove, Ill.: Albert Whitman, 1989); A. Hoffman, *At Risk* (New York: Putnam, 1988).
14. *You See, I've Already Had a Life* (30 min.; School of Communications and Theatre, 16mm Film Library, 13th and Norris Streets, Annenberg Hall, Philadelphia, PA 19122).
15. *Time*, 8 January 1973, 136.
16. *Machina* (8 min.: Paris: Vartkes Cholakian, 1964); *The String Bean* (17 min.; New York: Contem, 1964); *Nahanni* (19 min.; New York: NFB Canada, 1962).
17. *Indian Summer* (28 min.; New York: McGraw-Hill, 1964); *Geronimo Jones* (21 min.; New York: Learning Corp. of America, 1972); *Adventures of an ** (11 min.; New York: Macmillan Films, 1957); Shel Silverstein, *The Giving Tree* (New York: Harper & Row, 1964); Robert Munsch, *Love You Forever* (1986; Willowdale, Ont.: Firefly, 1991); F. Haskins, *Things I Like About Grandma* (San Francisco: Children's Book Press, 1992); M. Fox, *Wilfrid Gordon MacDonald Partridge* (New York: Omnibus, 1984).
18. It is fitting and proper to die for one's country (Horace).
19. *High Noon* (84 min.; Los Angeles: United Artists, 1952).
20. *Les Escargots* (15 min.; Paris: Les Filmes Armorial, 1965 / 1968); *Life Cycle* (8 min.; New York: NET, Dream Machine, 1972).

Index

Index

Index

Index